RA564.8 .V49 1991

Victor, Christina R.

Health and health care
in later life /
1991.

HEALTH AND HEALTH CARE
IN LATER LIFE

HEALTH AND HEALTH CARE
IN LATER LIFE

Christina R. Victor

310701
AF, 8905

Open University Press
Milton Keynes · Philadelphia

To David

Open University Press
Celtic Court
22 Ballmoor
Buckingham
MK18 1XW

and
1900 Frost Road, Suite 101
Bristol, PA 19007, USA

First Published 1991
Reprinted 1995

British Library Cataloguing-in-Publication Data

Victor, Christina
    Health and health care in later life.
    I. Title
    362.1084

    ISBN 0–335–09284–5
    ISBN 0–335–09283–7 (pbk)

Library of Congress Cataloging-in-Publication Data

Victor, Christina R.
    Health and health care in later life/Christina R. Victor.
        p.   cm.
    Includes index.
    ISBN 0–335–09284–5 (HB)   ISBN 0–335–09283–7 (PB)
    1. Aged–Health and hygiene.   2. Aged–Health and hygiene–Great
Britain.   I. Title.
    [DNLM: 1. Health Services for the Aged.   2. Health Status.
3. Mental Health–in old age.   WT 30 V642h]
RA564.8.V49   1991
362.1'9897–dc20
DNLM/DLC
for Library of Congress   91–2692 CIP

Typeset by Vision Typesetting
Printed and bound in Great Britain by
Biddles Ltd, Guildford and King's Lynn

CONTENTS

ACKNOWLEDGEMENTS

The data presented in this volume originate from a variety of different sources and it is my pleasure to formally thank all those who have made data available. I wish to thank the Office of Population Censuses and Surveys for granting access to the General Household Survey data. Access to these data and the Health and Lifestyle Survey was facilitated by the ESRC data archive at the University of Essex.

On a more personal level I thank my husband David Jefferies for his advice, encouragement and support during the writing of this volume. He introduced me to the mysteries of computer graphics and was a patient computer engineer when I was faced with the inevitable computer-related disasters of corrupting and incompatible disks!

1 INTRODUCTION

Modern Britain, in common with other western industrial countries, is experiencing population ageing. Population ageing refers to the changing age distribution of the population at an aggregate level and is, of course, distinct from individual ageing. Those aged 65 and over, the age usually taken as indicating the start of the later phases of the life cycle, now represent about 15 per cent of the total population compared with 5 per cent at the turn of the century. If current demographic patterns continue then the early decades of the next millennium will see a further numerical increase, but not necessarily a percentage increase, in this age group. This demographic revolution, which is discussed in more detail in Chapter 2, is heralded not as a triumph of public health but as an indication of impending social, economic and political disaster. Why is this?

Several factors explain the very negative way that population ageing is perceived. Old age on an individual level, however it is defined, is evaluated very negatively. The imagery associated with later life is centred upon stereotypes of physical decline and the financial and social 'burden' of supporting older people. Those in the older age groups are depicted as parasites upon the rest of society; a group which consumes resources without making a reciprocal contribution. These potent images are translated to the population level leading to the development of a 'moral panic' about the implications of population.

One area where this imagery of burden and decline is especially potent is that of ageing and health and the provision of health and social care services. Old age is inevitably associated with biological and physical decline. It is taken as quite natural that old age is a time of biological decline, which results in the entire population of older people being characterized by ill health and sickness. To be old is to be unhealthy. Given the widespread acceptance of this stereotype population ageing is presented as a 'social problem' because of concerns about society's ability to 'afford' to provide health and social welfare services for the increasing numbers of older people. The twin aims of this book are to look at the reality of these two popular scenarios at a population scale of analysis. These are ambitious objectives which are probably beyond the scope of a single book. Consequently the arguments and data advanced in this volume should be viewed as essentially descriptive and preliminary in approach. The analysis presented is an attempt to consider the way that health and disease are distributed within the older age groups and to consider how different this is from the pattern illustrated by other age groups. This is then compared with the provision of health and social care to older people and how this may (or may not) change with the impending implementation of radical changes in our health and social care system.

Ageing and health

First it is important to define what is meant by health within the limitations of this volume. There is no simple definition of health which is easily measured at the population level of analysis. Health may be conceptualized in a variety of ways including the absence of specific disease states or as a state of mind. It is misleading to think of a specific definition of health as 'the right one'. Health is clearly a complex and multifactorial entity. In this volume a variety of different approaches to measuring health status in later life are used. The justification for this is to try to provide a comprehensive overview of the different dimensions of health for the older age groups. Consequently the book includes material about specific conditions (e.g. dementia and incontinence), about particular categories of condition (e.g. chronic disability) and about older people's views about what constitutes health for them.

A feature of recent debates about health has been the focus upon the influence of lifestyle upon the distribution of health and illness within populations. It is not at all clear what is meant when social commentators refer to the influence of lifestyle upon health. Typically such debates centre around the choices individuals make which are related to known risk factors such as smoking, alcohol consumption and diet. However, such individual elements of behaviour are culturally and economically determined, and the determining factors also have an independent influence upon health status. In this book we also attempt to examine the lifestyle characteristics of the older age groups – an aspect which has long been neglected. Although we focus upon individual behaviour such as smoking the cultural and economic context within which such behaviour takes place must not be ignored.

METHODOLOGICAL CONSIDERATIONS

The prime objective of gerontological research is the identification and explanation of age based differences. In this book we are interested in research which has investigated the relationship between ageing and health. This rather simple objective is, in fact, highly problematic. Observed differences between age groups in, for example, the prevalence of dementia or chronic ill health, may reflect either the effects of ageing or cohort changes.

Age effects are changes which are attributable to changes in maturation or experience which result from biological ageing. We may, in theory at least, identify two types of age effects: intrinsic and reactive. Intrinsic age effects are changes which naturally, universally and inevitably accompany the ageing process regardless of the social context. Reactive age effects are those which are fashioned by the social environment. Such effects are, therefore, both culturally and historically specific. Although these two types of age effects are conceptually distinct, in practice it is often difficult to distinguish between them. Indeed, it is very difficult to identify age effects of either type because of methodological limitations.

Cohort or generational effects result from the influence of historical time and events upon a group of individuals born at roughly the same time. Differences observed between age groups or generations in, for example, mental functioning may simply reflect differences in educational opportunities between different generations and not the effect of decreasing mental functioning due to 'ageing'. Again, cohort effects may operate in two main ways. Some historical events may be experienced by one generation and not by succeeding cohorts. Those who were aged 75 in 1990 were born in 1915. This means that they experienced the First World War as small children, lived through the depression as young adults, served in the Second World War and saw the creation of the British welfare state in the post-war period. These experiences may be contrasted with those of a person born in 1946 who has experienced a (relatively) peaceful world, the post-war welfare state and the prosperity of the post-war years. The second aspect of the cohort effect is that the same event will be experienced by different cohorts in varying ways. The experience of living through the Second World War will vary according to whether the individual was in the cohort of school children, young adults or older people. In terms of health care the major cohort influences in Britain are the availability of free health care after the creation of the National Health Service (NHS) in 1948. Improvements in living standards and housing across the generations are probably also very important determinants of health status.

For the gerontologist, who is interested in changes over time or in identifying the effects of ageing, longitudinal studies are the most appropriate methodological approach. These studies involve the collection of data from the same group of subjects at several different points in time. For example, a researcher may follow up a population to see how many develop chronic health problems or various types of cancer after exposure to contraceptive pill use. The principle of the longitudinal study is the follow up of a study group over several years, with data being collected at regular intervals.

While this is the most appropriate way of studying ageing from a methodological perspective these types of studies do have inherent problems, including the practicalities of following up subjects over time, a costly procedure in terms of both time and resources. Participation in such a study may require considerable commitment from the study population; this may lead many potential subjects to refuse to participate, thereby biasing the results. Death may reduce the number in such studies significantly. Furthermore, if the researcher is interested in a rare disease then very large sample sizes may be required. However, if the objective of the research is to identify the effects of ageing then this is, in theory at least, the most appropriate methodology.

A cross-sectional study or approach involves comparing different age groups of people at a single point in time. In looking at health we may compute the number of times people of different ages consulted their doctor. Using this approach any differences observed between the groups may cautiously be attributed to ageing. The implicit assumption underlying this approach is that observing people of different ages at a single point in time has the same effect as observing one group over a period of time. Drawing inferences about the effects of ageing from cross-sectional data is problematic because differences between age groups may reflect cohort as well as age effects.

In reviewing the literature concerned with ageing and health most of the data are derived from cross-sectional research studies. Although differences identified are cautiously attributed to ageing in this book readers are cautioned to bear in mind the methodological deficiencies of much of the research base. There are few longitudinal studies of ageing and the utility of some of these may be questioned. Several studies are based upon volunteer samples and may not be representative of the general population. Consequently we must also be cautious in drawing inferences from longitudinal studies as their generalizability may be low.

Describing disease in populations

There are several reasons for examining the distribution and determinants of diseases within populations. These may be considered as either the search for causes or for information to assist the planning, development and evaluation of services. In seeking to understand the distribution of health and disease within older age groups some basic understanding of epidemiological terms is required. In describing the distribution of disease both within and between populations two key terms, prevalence and incidence, are used (see Table 1.1).

PREVALENCE

The prevalence of a disease is the number of cases of, for example, senile dementia or hip disease, in a given population at a specific point in time. The notion of prevalence is based upon the assumption that populations may be divided simply into cases (i.e. those who have the disease) and non-cases (i.e. those without the disease). The number with the disease is then divided by the

Table 1.1 Describing disease in populations.

A Prevalence: the proportion of the population suffering from the disorder measured

$$= \frac{\text{number with disorder at stated time}}{\text{total population}} \times 1000$$

e.g. = prevalence of osteo-arthritis in population aged 65 +

$$= \frac{\text{number with osteo-arthritis}}{\text{total population aged 65 +}} \times 1000$$

B Incidence: rate of occurrence of new cases

$$= \frac{\text{number of new cases of a disorder in a given population over specific time period}}{\text{population at risk in given time}} \times 1000$$

e.g. = annual incidence of osteo-arthritis in population aged 65 +

$$= \frac{\text{number of new cases in population aged 65 + and 1 year}}{\text{average number of people aged 65 + in year}} \times 1000$$

population at risk. Multiplication of the result by 1000 produces the prevalence rate.

The assumption of a simple dichotomy of diseases into present and absent and the clear distinction between cases and non-cases is problematic when studying conditions such as disability. Chronic diseases do not have a simple cut-off point at which someone may be unambiguously classified as disabled or demented. For many diseases there is a continuum which ranges in intensity from slight to severe. The level or threshold selected as the cut off to define a case of dementia will obviously influence the resultant prevalence estimate (see Figure 1.1). Moving the case definition threshold from $d1$ to $d2$ will increase the number of people classed as disabled and so increase the prevalence estimate.

INCIDENCE

The incidence of a disease refers to the number of new cases occurring in a given population within a defined period of time, e.g. one year. This statistic is dependent upon the accurate and comprehensive identification of new cases of the disease under consideration. This statistic is, like prevalence, sensitive to the definition of what is and is not a case of the disease under consideration. However, the study of incidence rates is further complicated by the need to identify the point of onset. With many of the diseases of later life it is not always obvious when the onset of a specific condition occurred. Studies of incidence based upon first presentation to services will obviously under-estimate the true incidence of a specific condition.

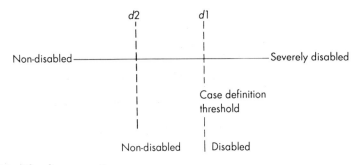

Fig. 1.1 The disease continuum.

THE RELATIONSHIP BETWEEN INCIDENCE AND PREVALENCE

The incidence and prevalence rates for any disease are clearly interrelated. The prevalence of any disorder is dependent upon:

1 The incidence rate.
2 Length of survival after the onset of the disease.
3 The size of the population at risk.

Thus it is important not to simply study incidence but to try to establish survival rates. This is, however, not easy. In trying to predict the future demands for care resultant from, for example, dementia, it is usual to project forward current prevalence rates. This is a very approximate way of predicting demands for care because it assumes the continuation of current incidence and survival rates. Consequently we must be aware of the limitations of this approach when considering future patterns of (ill) health within the older age groups.

RATES AND STANDARDIZATION

Having identified the number of people with a specific condition there are a number of different ways of describing this information. Taking the example of deaths, we can calculate the crude death rate; this is the number of deaths per 1000 total population at risk. This statistic presents only a very superficial overview of the health status of a population so it is usual to calculate age and sex specific rates. For example, we can look at death rates for men and women separately and for three specific age groups; 65–74, 75–84 and 85 and over. Detailed age and sex specific rates can only be calculated if we have detailed information about the population at risk in these different subdivisions. Such data are not always available.

Comparison of crude rates between populations or over time may be problematic. A change in crude death rates may simply reflect a change in the age and sex composition of the population. Identification of differences in death rates between social classes may simply reflect the younger age of the professional and managerial classes. A statistical procedure known as standardization is used to take into account differences in age, sex or other socio-demographic variables (or indeed combinations of such variables) between populations which are being compared. Put at its crudest, this method entails applying age–specific mortality rates to the study population in order to derive an expected number of deaths (or disabled people). The observed number of deaths is then compared with the expected number and a ratio produced. A standardized mortality ratio (SMR) of 100 indicates that the observed mortality of a population is the same as expected; a rate in excess of 100 indicates excess mortality and less than 100 suggests lower than expected mortality. Although the example given relates to mortality the procedure of standardization may be applied to a variety of factors, including morbidity and service utilization.

The policy context: developments in health and social care

Any debate about the provision of care for older people (or indeed any other segment of the population) takes place within the context of major changes in the provision of these services resultant from the passing of the Health and Community Care Bill in June 1990. Before considering these changes we need to present a brief summary of the arrangements for the provision of health and social care before the implementation of these changes.

THE PHILOSOPHY OF THE NHS

Under the welfare state arrangements established after the end of the Second World War Britain has a socialized system of health care; the National Health Service (NHS). The NHS came into existence on 5 July 1948 and was intended to provide a comprehensive range of care to all those who required it. The service is available to consumers free at the point of consumption and is largely funded from general taxation. The prime objective of the NHS is the provision of an equitable health care service, accessible to all citizens of Britain regardless of where they live or of their financial and personal circumstances.

THE CREATION OF THE NHS

When the NHS was created there were three main existing types of hospital provision: public hospitals which developed from the workhouse infirmaries: voluntary/charitable; and private. Standards of care were generally higher in the voluntary hospitals than in the public sector. This is because the voluntary hospitals 'chose' the patients that they would treat and generally favoured those with acute health problems. Care of the chronic sick, elderly and those with mental health problems was generally left to the public sector. In addition to hospital services there were the general practitioners (GPs) and the community nursing services which were run by the local authorities. The 1948 NHS was based upon the existing pattern of provision and a tripartite system of administration was established to reflect this. Doyal (1979) describes this as the nationalization of existing health provision rather than the creation of a truly socialized system of provision. Further details about the structure of the NHS can be found elsewhere (Ham 1985; Lethard 1990).

THE NHS IN CRISIS: DEBATES ABOUT RESOURCES AND MANAGEMENT

Since the creation of the NHS two key themes have dominated debates about the future of the service: finance/resources and management/administration. Each of these is briefly considered below.

Perhaps the key assumption upon which the NHS had been planned was the notion that there was a 'fixed' amount of illness in the community which the NHS would gradually diminish. Consequently it was assumed that expenditure on the NHS would eventually diminish and level off once existing diseases had been eliminated. It soon became evident that this was a false premise and expenditure on the NHS increased steadily (Ham 1985). At 1949 prices, expenditure per capita on health care increased from £437 in 1949 to £1490 in 1984. In 1949 total expenditure on the NHS was £437 million; by 1984 this had risen to £16,695 million (Ham 1985). The cost of the services has increased threefold in real terms and it now represents 6.2 per cent of gross national product as compared with 3.9 per cent in 1948. These expenditure increases prompted the following comment from the Royal Commission on the NHS: 'the demand for health care is always likely to outstrip supply ... the capacity of health services to absorb resources is almost unlimited' (Royal Commission on the NHS 1979, p. 51).

As well as concern about resources the history of the NHS has been characterized by worries about coordination between the different arms of the service and the way the system has been managed (Ham 1985). The NHS has been subject to managerial restructuring in 1974, 1982 and 1985. This last reorganization saw the introduction of general management into the administration of health care.

The aims of successive reorganizations have consistently been to improve collaboration between the different elements of the health and social care system, to integrate all health service administration within the NHS and improve the management of the system at all levels. The introduction of business-style general management may be seen as the culmination of a trend which has characterized the NHS since its inception; the identification of the 'problems' of the NHS as essentially managerial rather than, for example, as arising from inadequate resources. Each successive reorganization has sought to 'solve' the perceived problems of the NHS by the introduction of 'better' management.

THE CURRENT STRUCTURE OF THE NHS PRIOR TO APRIL 1991

The pre-April 1991 structure of the NHS was based upon the 1982 reorganization. Following the 1979 Consultative document *Patients First* the NHS was again reorganized in 1982 and consisted, in England, of 14 regional health authorities (RHAs) and 192 district health authorities (DHAs) (see Figure 1.2). Amalgamations have now reduced the number of DHAs to 189. The DHA was responsible for the provision of health services to meet the needs of their local population. Administratively the DHA was responsible for the provision of hospital care and community health services such as health visiting and community nursing. Under the arrangements for health care provision current in 1990 the DHA was not responsible for the provision of general practitioner (GP) services. Within the National Health Service the general practitioners (GPs) are independent contractors. This means that they did not become salaried employees of the NHS but held individual contracts which were administered via the executive council (the family practitioner) committee (FPC)) and now renamed the Family Health Service Authority (FHSA). The FPC has responsibility for the payment of GPs and some aspects of the organization of the services, but has little power to influence the planning and organization of services. With the inception of the NHS the GPs retained the right to be paid upon the basis of number of patients registered rather than receive an annual salary. This reflects a continuity with the pre-NHS system when GPs maintained a panel or list of patients which formed the basis of their remuneration. The development of the GP service has been coloured by the independent status of GPs. This has meant that the NHS has had no power to match the supply of family doctors with areas of demand. Consequently provision of GP services has been patchy, standards of care have varied between areas and recommendations such as the development of health centres have had only limited impact.

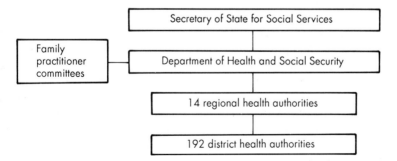

Fig. 1.2 Organization of the National Health Service, 1982–90.

WORKING FOR PATIENTS: THE 1988 NHS REVIEW

The 1988 review of the NHS, which was published as the White Paper *Working for Patients* in January 1989 was prompted by a concern over the underfunding of the service (DOH 1989a). The White Paper came up with a managerial rather than resource-increase solution to the problem. The proposals contained in this document are consistent with government ideology in that it attempts to apply market principles to the institution which is the cornerstone of the British welfare state. These reforms are to come into operation in April 1991.

The 1988 review of the NHS was widely seen as a spontaneous response by the prime minister to a perceived crisis in the funding of the NHS which attracted considerable media attention in the winter of 1987/88. This crisis centred around issues of funding and the adequacy of levels of expenditure. The review, which formed the basis of the subsequent White Paper, took one year to complete and was an entirely internal exercise. Public consultations were not invited.

The NHS White Paper claims two main objectives:

1 To give patients, irrespective of area of residence, better health care and a greater choice of service.
2 To provide greater satisfaction and rewards to those working in the NHS who respond to local needs and preferences.

The document proposes a number of changes in the way the NHS is organized. The eight key measures put forward to achieve these two objectives are as follows:

1 To devolve as much responsibility as possible to the local (i.e. hospital or DHA) level in order to promote a more responsive service.
2 The creation of autonomous hospital trusts within NHS hospitals which opt out in order to stimulate better patient services. These trusts will take full responsibility for their own affairs including conditions and rates of pay for staff. They will be able to earn money by selling their services to other hospitals and health authorities.
3 The creation of an internal market within the NHS by the separation of those who purchase and those who provide care. The providing agencies will consist of all directly managed NHS hospitals and community services, NHS trust hospitals and private sector hospitals. The purchasing agencies will be district health authorities and those GPs who opt to become direct budget holders. The DHA and its agencies will be responsible for the purchase of appropriate health care which meet the needs of their population. DHAs, and budget holding GPs, will be able to purchase care from other districts, hospitals and the private sector. The assumption is that competition between providers will improve the range and quality of patient services and improve value for money.
4 Creation of 100 new consultant posts over three years to reduce hours

worked by junior doctors, reduce waiting times and improve the appointment system.

5 Management at national, regional and DHA/FHSA level to be reformed. Membership of these bodies will be reduced in size and, like businesses, will include executive and non-executive directors.

6 The development of medical audit to ensure that services are providing value for money and are of the highest quality.

7 Large GP practices above 9000 patients (11,000 in the initial policy document) to hold their own budgets to obtain a defined range of services directly from hospitals. GPs will be encouraged to compete for patients by offering better services and it will become easier for patients to change their GP.

8 The funding of DHAs on a capitation basis. Currently there is no direct relationship between the amount of money a district receives and the number of patients treated. Under the reforms districts will be funded according to their population size, health and age distribution, especially the number of elderly patients. Hospital provider units will not be directly funded as at present. Rather these units will have to source their funds from the DHAs in which the patients they treat reside.

CHANGES IN PRIMARY CARE

Alongside the NHS changes there have been important changes in the operation of primary care. Following the 1987 White Paper *Promoting Better Health* a new GP contract was imposed upon family doctors by the Department of Health and came into force in April 1990. The stated objective of this new contract is to improve the standard of general practice and it proposes substantial changes in the way general practice is structured and financed. The item which is of most concern to older people is the imposition upon family doctors of an obligation to offer screening annually to all their patients aged 75+.

SOCIAL AND COMMUNITY CARE

The remit of the DHA is the provision of health care and the FHSA takes responsibility for primary care services. There is no such neat division of responsibility for social care. Very loosely this may be defined as continuing care which is required to maintain individuals in the community. A variety of different agencies are involved in the provision of this type of care (see Table 1.2). The statutory sector provides services such as home care, day centres, residential care and social work. These services are provided by the local authority social services departments which were created under the 1974 local government reorganization. The local authority is an elected body whose housing departments are also involved in social care by the provision of sheltered housing. Private and voluntary agencies are also involved.

Table 1.2 Main community care services for older people.

Agency	Service
Health authority	Hospitals – acute
	Hospitals – long stay
	Community nursing
	Community rehabilitation
	Day hospitals
Family practitioner committee	GPs
	Dental services
	Ophthalmic services
Social services	Residential homes
	Day centres
	Social work
	Good neighbour schemes
	Street warden
	Home helps
Housing authorities	Sheltered housing
Housing associations	Sheltered housing
Voluntary sector	Residential homes
	Nursing homes
	Sheltered housing
	Lunch clubs
	Mobile meals services
	Volunteers/good neighbours
Private sector	Nursing homes
	Residential homes
	Sheltered housing
	Domestic agencies

There has been a broad consensus about the appropriateness of community care as a social policy objective. However, it has not been seen to be a very effective set of policies. So this policy has been subject to recent rigorous scrutiny by a series of government reports; the Audit Commission (1986), the House of Commons Social Services Committee Report (1985) and the Griffiths Report 'Community care: agenda for action' (DHSS 1986) which resulted in the 1989 White Paper *Caring for People* (DOH 1989b). (This White Paper is subsequently referred to as the Griffiths White Paper.) The entire document is based upon the assumption that it is possible to divide the population into two groups: those with social care needs and those with health care needs. The latter group remain under the jurisdiction of the health agencies while those with social care needs will be catered for by local authority social service departments.

The White Paper states that the proposed changes are intended to:

• enable people to live as normal a life as possible in their own homes or in a homely environment in the community;

- provide the right amount of care and support to enable people to achieve maximum independence;
- provide people with greater say in how they live their lives and the services they need.

The key recommendations of this White Paper are summarized briefly as follows:

1 Local authorities should be the lead agency in developing community care with the responsibility for assessing the needs of individuals for care and developing an appropriate package of services within the resources available.
2 Local authorities are required to publish clear plans for the development of community care services.
3 A mixed economy of welfare provision should be developed, using the private, voluntary and public sectors. There is to be a split between those parts of the local authority which directly provide care for clients (providing agencies) and those which purchase care for clients (purchasing authorities).
4 Local authorities are to be responsible for the provision of social care while medical care remains the province of the NHS.
5 New funding arrangements will mean that local authorities will manage a social care budget regardless of whether the care is provided at home or in an institution.
6 There should be a single method of entry for those being supported by public funds irrespective of the type of institution (i.e. public, private, voluntary) which they wished to enter.
7 The distinction between sectors in terms of standards and regulatory procedures should be abolished with a single set of standards for all residential facilities.

These reforms were initially intended to be implemented in April 1991 but implementation is now being phased in over three years.

Conclusion

This book has two main themes. The first relates to the description of the health status of older people; the second considers health and social care for older people. Given the twin aims of the book the rest of the volume is divided into two main parts. The first part considers the health status of the older age groups by examining patterns of mortality (Chapter 3), morbidity (Chapter 4), mental health (Chapter 5) and health beliefs and lifestyle (Chapter 6). Before examining the health status the first chapter of this section considers the demographic and social characteristics of the older age groups as this provides the context within which to discuss health status. In the second part of the book we concentrate upon the utilization of health (Chapter 7) and social care services (Chapter 8). The book concludes by considering how changes in services resulting from recent policy reviews may affect the care provided for older people.

2 THE DEMOGRAPHIC CONTEXT

The greying of the British population is presented as one of the major challenges of the coming decades. This concern has been manifest in the debate over intergenerational conflict about access to resources. Questions have been posed about the willingness (or otherwise) of future generations of working age to support those who have retired from formal employment (Johnson *et al.* 1989). Such concerns have been manifest in the reforms of social security pursued by Conservative administration in Britain in the 1980s. The documents which preceded the reforms showed a widespread concern with the relationship between the number of those available to pay national insurance contributions and the recipients of the benefits provided. These debates are outside the scope of this volume, although some aspects of the perceived burden of supporting older people will be raised in the chapters concerned with the health status of the older age groups and issues relating to the supply and consumption of formal and informal care.

The issue of population ageing is central to the consideration of current arrangements for the provision of care by formal services. It also provides the context for the reviews of community care, NHS provision and arrangements for primary care. Such debates consider the older age groups as a uniform social group with a homogeneous set of needs for health and social care. This chapter is divided into three main sections. The first presents an overview of the main demographic trends in Britain during this century and attempts to provide a considered overview of these population changes. The second part of the chapter considers the main demographic and household characteristics of the population aged 65 + as these also are important when considering aspects of health status in later life and the need for health and social care. In the final part of the chapter the focus of attention is upon the social circumstances of this age group. Where possible comparisons are made with older countries, especially those of western Europe, as this enables us to identify the uniqueness (or otherwise) of the trends observed in Britain.

Population ageing in Great Britain

In looking at population ageing we will consider two distinct dimensions. First we examine the trends in population structure in Britain over the last century and the forecasts for the early decades of the next millennium. In the second section the focus of attention is upon the statistical methods used to describe population structures.

POPULATION TRENDS 1901–2025

In 1988 the estimated population of the United Kingdom was 57.1 million (CSO 1990) of whom 8.9 million, or 15 per cent of the total population, were aged 65 years or older. During the twentieth century Britain, in common with most industrial western societies, has undergone a major demographic transformation (OECD 1988). There are two main factors underlying this change in the nature of the population distribution: decreased mortality and reduced fertility. In England and Wales the crude death rate for the period 1840–45 was 21.4 per 1000 population; for 1980–85 the equivalent rate was 11.8 per 1000 (OPCS 1989a). The most spectacular change in mortality rates over the past 150 years has related to deaths within the first year of life – the infant mortality rate. In 1840–45 the infant mortality rate for England and Wales was 148 per 1000 live births compared with 9 per 1000 in 1980–85 (OPCS 1989a). In addition there have been significant decreases in fertility over the same period. In 1900 the crude fertility rate, the number of births per 1000 population, was 27 per 1000 (Tinker 1984) compared with 13.8 per 1000 in 1988 (CSO 1990). Consequently decreased mortality among all ages (but especially in the first year of life), together with a long-term reduction in fertility, have combined to produce an ageing population structure. This means that the proportion of younger people within the population is decreasing while the proportion of older people is increasing. The traditional demographic structure, which was pyramid-like in shape, with a wide base (indicating a large number of young people) and narrow top (indicating few people in the older age groups), has been replaced by a more equal distribution among the different age groups.

Before the onset of the 1939–45 world war little concern had been expressed about the rapid decline in fertility in Britain and the consequent ageing of the population. The first real awareness of the changing population structure and the development of the view of population ageing as 'a bad thing' is contained in the 1949 Royal Commission of Population. This document put forward the now stereotypical view that a population with a decreasing number of young people in it would be unprogressive and less vigorous than other nations. The negative attributes of old age at an individual level were, for the first time, being applied to the population as a whole. The notion of the older age groups as an economic burden posing a threat to the economic standards of other members of the population is illustrated by the report of the Phillips Committee in 1954

Table 2.1 Number (in millions) and proportion of elderly people in the population of Great Britian, 1901–2025.

	65–74	75–84	85+	% total aged 65+
1901	1.2	0.5	0.05	4.7
1951	3.7	1.6	0.2	10.9
1961	4.0	1.9	0.3	11.8
1971	4.8	2.2	0.5	13.2
1981	5.2	2.7	0.6	15.0
1991	5.0	3.1	0.9	
2001	4.8	3.2	1.2	
2011	5.2	3.1	1.3	
2025	6.0	3.9	1.4	

Source: CSO (1989), Table 1.2.

which was first to raise the alarm about the prospective costs of providing pensions for future generations of elderly.

The number of people aged 65 and over in Great Britain increased from 1.75 million in 1901 to 8.5 million in 1981. This absolute increase has also been reflected in an increase in the percentage of total population accounted for by those aged 65+. In 1901 5 per cent of the population was aged over 65 compared with 15 per cent aged 65 in 1981 (see Table 2.1).

The population of Great Britain is increasing although the rate of increase is lower than at earlier times in our history. Current forecasts predict that the population of the United Kingdom will increase to approximately 61 million by the year 2025 (CSO 1990). Such forecasts are, however, only predictions and are based upon the extrapolation of current trends in both mortality and fertility. Forecasts of mortality are now reasonably accurate. Fertility is a much more difficult aspect of human behaviour to predict!

These demographic forecasts for the numbers of older people are much more reliable as these people are already born. Current forecasts indicate, with the exception of a slight decrease around the turn of the millennium, that the population aged over 65 will continue to increase from 8.8 million in 1987 to 11.3 million in 2025 (see Table 2.1).

The number of people in the 65–74 age group is predicted to increase from 5.2 million in 1981 to 6 million by 2025. The largest proportionate increases are expected among those aged over 85 years: from 0.8 million (1987) to 1.4 million (2025), an increase of 42 per cent. It is the large percentage increases in the very elderly age groups which constitute the data used to create an almost 'moral panic' about population ageing. However, examination of the actual numerical increases indicate that the number aged 85+ will increase by about 800,000.

Population ageing is operating at two distinct levels: societal and within the older age groups itself. In 1901 2 per cent of those aged 65+ were aged over

85; by the year 2025 this will have increased to 12 per cent. However, the very elderly still only represent a minority, approximately 1 per cent of the total population.

It is fairly unproblematic to predict the number of older people in the population at future points in time. These individuals are already born and we may fairly accurately estimate mortality for different age and sex groups. However, predicting what proportion of the total population the older age groups (or any other subset of the population) will represent is more problematic as it depends upon the number of children future generations produce. The birth rate is notoriously difficult to predict as people remain very capricious in their decisions about when, and how many, children to have. Hence all predictions about what proportion of the total population the 65 + age group will constitute in the future are little more than speculations based upon the extrapolation of current trends. To overcome this problem many policy papers which examine population ageing produce a variety of projections using different fertility assumptions. Although we can state what percentage of total population the older age groups currently represent, it is not reliable to quote future percentages; such predictions should be treated with the utmost caution.

Population ageing is not unique to Britain but is a characteristic feature of most western industrial societies and, increasingly the less developed parts of the world. Scott and Johnson (1988) report that in 1980 8.5 per cent of the world's population was aged 60 years or over; by 2025 this is expected, if current trends persist, to increase to 13.7 per cent. Among the developed countries of the world 11 per cent of the population are over 65, compared with about 4 per cent in the developing nations (Laslett 1989). In demographic terms the developed countries are old societies, whereas the developing world has a youthful population structure. More specifically Europe is the oldest of all the continents. Among 14 countries of Europe, North America and Australasia trends in population structure are very similar (Table 2.2). For example in Great Britain the percentage of the population aged 65 and over was 5 per cent in 1901 and 15 per cent in 1985. During the same period in New Zealand this age group increased from 2 per cent to 10 per cent of total population.

POPULATION DEPENDENCY RATIOS

Of obvious importance within individual societies is the relationship between the different age groups as this has considerable implications for the development of health and social policy and economic development. For example, a young society will need educational infrastructures. As has already been hinted, many western countries are concerned about the ageing of their populations, largely because of issues relating to the perceived burden of financially supporting older people and their high use of health and social services.

Table 2.2   Percentage of total population aged 65, in 14 countries, 1901 and 1985.

| | % of total population | |
	1901	1985
Canada	5	10
USA	4	12
Australia	5	14
Belgium	6	14
Denmark	7	15
France	8	13
Germany	5	15
Great Britain	5	15
Netherlands	6	12
Norway	8	16
Sweden	8	17
Switzerland	6	14
Australia	4	10
New Zealand	2	10

Source: Scott and Johnson (1988), Table 1.3.

There is an obvious need to be able to develop indicators which summarize the structure of a given population at a variety of scales of analysis (e.g national, regional or county). Several different methods are available to describe the age distribution of populations and the relationship between its constituent age groups. One of the most frequently cited indices is what is termed the 'dependency ratio'. This is the ratio of the combination of those aged 65 + (or whatever age is taken as a proxy for entry into later life) and those aged 0–15 to those of working age (i.e. 16–64). The overall dependency ratio may be subdivided into two constituent elements; the elderly dependency ratio, known in the USA as the 'gerontic' dependency ratio, and the youth dependency, or 'neontic', ratio. Examples of the method of calculation of these indicators are shown in Table 2.3.

Much of this moral panic about population ageing seems to have developed from the widespread and possibly indiscriminate use of population dependency ratios (Calasanti and Bonanno 1986). In 1980 the overall dependency ratio in Britain was 56.2 and it is predicted to increase to 56.7 by the year 2020 (Table 2.4). The increase in the elderly dependency ratio over the same period was from 23.2 to 25.5; a rate of increase considerably less than that likely to be experienced by many other developed countries. Comparison of the patterns of demographic change suggested by the overall and gerontic ratio illustrates the importance of looking at both the total population and its component segments. For example, the overall dependency ratio for Canada is projected to decrease by 3 per cent between 1980 and 2020; this masks a predicted 205 per cent increase in the gerontic ratio over the same period.

One feature of the use of both dependency ratios and population projections

Table 2.3 Summarizing population structures.

1 Method of calculation
(a) Dependency ratio

$$= \frac{\text{population aged } 0\text{--}15 + \text{population aged } 65+}{\text{population aged } 16\text{--}64} \times 100$$

(b) Gerontic dependency ratio

$$= \frac{\text{population aged } 65+}{\text{population aged } 16\text{--}64} \times 100$$

(c) Neontic dependency ratio

$$= \frac{\text{population aged } 0\text{--}15}{\text{population aged } 16\text{--}64} \times 100$$

2 Worked example: United Kingdom 1988 (all figures in millions)
(a) Dependency ratio

$$= \frac{11.5 + 8.9}{36.6} = \frac{20.4}{36.6} = 0.56 \times 100$$

$$= 56$$

(b) Gerontic dependency ratio

$$= \frac{8.9}{36.6} = 0.24 \times 100$$

$$= 24$$

(c) Neontic dependency ratio

$$= \frac{11.5}{36.6} = 0.31 \times 100$$

$$= 31$$

Source: CSO (1990), Table 1.2.

Table 2.4 Dependency ratios for seven countries, 1980 and 2020.

	All ages			Gerontic		
	1980	*2020*	*% change*	*1980*	*2020*	*% change*
UK	56.2	56.7	+1	23.2	25.5	+10
Canada	48.1	46.6	−3	14.1	28.9	+205
France	56.8	57.3	+1	21.9	30.6	+40
Germany	50.8	54.3	+7	23.4	33.5	+43
Italy	54.9	51.5	−6	20.8	29.3	+41
Japan	48.4	60.6	+25	13.5	33.6	+249
USA	52.3	50.7	−3	17.1	25.0	+46

Source: OECD (1988), Tables 13 and 14.

is that they concentrate upon expected changes in structures. By definition they do not look backwards at the kinds of demographic transformations with which various societies have already coped. Such a solely prospective perspective promotes the impression that large percentage increases in, for example, the very old (i.e. those aged 85 +) are a new experience which is unique to the next three decades. Careful examination of Table 2.1 suggests that this is not the case. The interwar years in Britain were characterized by large percentage increases in the population aged 85 +. Similarly in both Britain and the United States overall dependency ratios were highest in the immediate post-war period, as a result of the baby boom. Overall dependency ratios are projected to be at their lowest in the United States in 2010 (Binney and Estes 1988).

Indices such as the dependency ratio are widely quoted and are of some use in portraying overall trends and relationships between different elements of the population of specific countries (or any other geographical area). They are also of interest in enabling the demographic profile of countries to be directly compared. However, their meaningful interpretation is problematic for two reasons: methods of calculation and assumptions.

Calculating dependency ratios retrospectively or for current circumstances is not problematic. The data are readily available in most developed countries. However, while it may be legitimate to calculate such indices upon the basis of known population figures, it is highly problematic to construct future projections of the ratios as they rest upon assumptions about future patterns of fertility which are almost impossible to predict. Consequently dependency ratios for future decades are again only best estimates and not real facts. They must be ascribed the status due to calculations which contain a large element of estimation.

More problematic than issues relating to the calculation of these statistics are the assumptions upon which they are based. The implicit assumptions upon which the ratios are based are contentious, value laden and rarely articulated. The main assumptions implicit within the dependency ratio are as follows:

- All those aged 0–15 and 65 + are 'dependent'.
- All those aged 16–64 are gainfully employed and contributing to the social welfare support of the two age extremes of the population.
- All members of the 'dependent population' are equally dependent and do not present varying social costs of support.

We will now consider the validity of these assumptions. First, the definition of the age of 65 years as initiating the onset of old age dependency is both arbitrary and socially constructed and is largely the result of institutionalized forced retirement. The implication of these types of ratio is that the population may be divided into two groups; assets, i.e. those who are gainfully employed or assumed to be so, and liabilities, those who are not contributing to society.

Second, the typical dependency ratio assumes that all those aged 16–64 are gainfully employed. How legitimate is this assumption? Falkingham (1989) has examined dependency ratios for Britain. She shows that to assume that all those aged 16–64 are economically active is a gross assumption unsupported by the available data. Economic activity rates vary between age and gender groups within the population; they also vary historically. For example, labour force participation rates for women have, until very recently, been low, so that in 1981 approximately 60 per cent of women between the ages of 20 and 59 were defined by the census as economically active. Factors such as unemployment and the number of young people attending further education also influence labour force participation rates. Clearly the assumption that all those within a specific age band are economically active is as naive as the assumption that all those above a certain age are inactive. A further difficulty relates to defining precisely what does and does not constitute economic activity.

For the United States Calasanti and Bonanno (1986) have calculated a dependency ratio using a number of different assumptions about female labour force participation. Excluding non-working women from the analysis altogether gives a ratio of 0.7, while including non-working women as dependent produces a ratio of 0.9. This analysis shows how sensitive these measures are to varying assumptions about unemployment and female labour for participation. They also show that, for the United States, the dependency ratio actually peaked in 1960 and is now decreasing because of the return of women to the workforce.

The third assumption of the dependency ratio is that those aged 65 + and those aged 0–15 are equally dependent; the ratio is not usually weighted in any way. Again this assumption is rather gross as the social and health care needs of the two age groups are rather different and the costs of supporting these two age groups are also very different.

The characteristics of the elderly population

What is loosely described as 'the elderly population' covers an age range from 65 to 100 + years and is not the homogeneous social group that this unitary term would indicate. This section considers some of the important demographic features of the older age groups which are of importance when considering future and current demands for health and social care.

SEX STRUCTURE

There is a marked gender inequality in the population aged 65 +. Later life is predominantly a female experience. Of the population aged 65 years and over 60 per cent are female (see Figure 2.1). This trend is at its most extreme among the very elderly (i.e. those aged 85 years or over) when there are 250 females for every 100 males. This may partly reflect a cohort or historical effect. The 'old old', i.e. those aged 85 and over, were born in the years 1890–1905. The

Population in millions

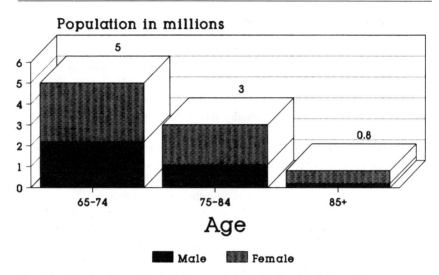

Fig. 2.1 Sex structure of population aged 65 + in Great Britain, 1986.
Source: CSO (1989), Table 1.2.

number of males surviving to old age in these birth cohorts has been very significantly deleted by the huge mortality associated with the 1914–18 world war.

The gender imbalance is seen by many as the natural order of things, indicating some form of biological superiority for women. However, this is a phenomenon of fairly recent origin. Up to the middle of last century life expectancy was greater among males than females due to the high mortality associated with child bearing (Victor 1987).

The reasons for the current gender imbalance are not fully understood. However, medical interventions have been relatively unsuccessful in decreasing the mortality of the diseases which are most common killers of middle-aged men, i.e. heart disease, strokes and other circulatory diseases. The higher rate of smoking among men, causing lung cancer and much heart disease, may partly explain the differential. The future effect of increased rates of smoking among women in the period since 1930 upon the gender division of the older age groups remains unknown. Our current evidence to explain the gender imbalance illustrated by the older age groups is very flimsy and is considered in more detail in Chapter 4.

This gender imbalance in later life is not a trend which is unique to Great Britain. The majority of people aged over 65 are female in a variety of western industrialized countries (Table 2.5). The percentage of the older age groups who are female has increased since the beginning of this century. This probably reflects the effect of high male mortality rates resultant from the major wars and it should not therefore be assumed that future cohorts of elderly will continue to

Table 2.5 Population aged 64 + who are female, in six countries (%), 1900–01 and 1985.

| | % population aged 64 + | |
	1900/01	*1985*
Australia	43	58
France	54	62
Italy	50	57
Germany	55	66
Great Britain	56	61
USA	50	60

Source: Scott and Johnson (1988), Table 1.4.

illustrate this extreme gender imbalance. Evidence to support this speculation is available from countries such as Japan where the gender imbalance is much less marked than the countries of western Europe.

MARITAL STATUS

As with other sections of the population those aged 65 + may be classified according to their civil status. This divides the population into four major groups: the legally married, widowed, single (i.e. never married) and divorced/legally separated. The civil status of older people in Britain varies with their sex. In 1981 there were marked differences in the marital status of men and women in the older age groups. At all ages over 65 women are less likely to be married than men; 78 per cent of all males aged 65 + were still married compared with 46 per cent of females. In contrast 50 per cent of women aged 65 + and 18 per cent of men are widowed. This difference in marital status increases with age; for those aged over 75 61 per cent of men are married compared with 21 per cent of women (Figure 2.2). This difference between the sexes in civil status reflects two interacting factors: the tendency for women to marry men older than themselves and the differential life expectancy of men and women. Widowhood is now something which is almost exclusively associated with later life. As Laslett (1989) points out there is an age in every population at which the widowed form a statistical majority. He shows that for men this occurs at an age somewhere in the mid-80s. For women it is much earlier in their early 70s. Changes in mortality have influenced the marital status composition of the older age groups in Britain over the last century. Falkingham (1987) has examined trends in marital status for the over-65s from 1901 to 1981. As death rates have declined the proportion of elderly classed as married has increased while the proportion widowed has decreased. In 1901 58 per cent of men aged 65 were married compared with 78 per cent in 1981; for women of the same age group the proportions classed as married at these two time points

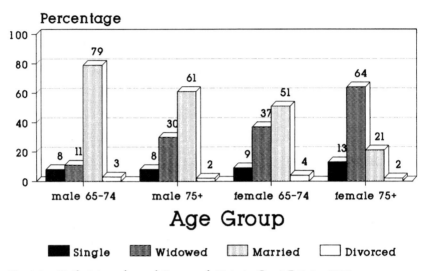

Fig. 2.2   Civil status of population aged 65 + in Great Britain, 1986.

were 38 per cent and 46 per cent respectively. In 1901 38 per cent of men were widowed compared with 18 per cent in 1981; for women the proportions were 50 per cent and 44 per cent respectively.

A substantial minority of Britain's population aged 65 + has never married. For men this is about 3 per cent and has remained constant. For women the never married group has always constituted a higher fraction of the older groups; in 1980 it was 9 per cent of those aged 65 +, while the peak was 1951 when it was 16.3 per cent. The large percentage of now elderly women who never married reflects an important cohort effect which was introduced earlier; the impact of the First World War. The high death rate among young men during the Great War of 1914–18 meant that a substantial number of women were unable to find partners to marry. Thus the high percentage of now elderly women who never married is not related to ageing; it is not an age effect. Rather this is a feature which is unique to that particular generation or cohort but which has profound implications for the provision of family care to older people in the community. It is very unlikely that future generations will exhibit this particular demographic characteristic. Another feature of the civil status distribution of the older age groups is the very small percentage of the older age groups classified as divorced. This again reflects the influence of historical time. For the current generations of older people divorce was neither easy to obtain nor socially acceptable. The effects of high divorce rates characteristic of the post-1960s in Britain upon family structures, filial responsibility and grandparent-hood remain largely unknown but will probably have a profound influence upon the experience of ageing for future generations of older people.

INSTITUTIONAL LIVING

A common image of later life is its association with residential care and institutional living. Approximately 3 per cent of those aged 65 and over live in some form of institution, either a residential home, nursing home or a long stay hospital bed. This is half the estimate for 1901. The percentage of older people living in institutional settings increases with age but is always very much lower than the percentage living in the community (Figure 2.3). Even among the very oldest old, those aged 85 and over, 19 per cent live in institutions. However, we can look at the obverse of this and state that 81 per cent live independently in the community. At all ages above 75 years women are more likely to be living in an institution than their male contemporaries.

In Britain it would appear that the percentage of those aged 65 + defined as living in some form of institution has remained constant or perhaps decreased slightly. Comparisons of the percentage of those aged 65 + living in communal establishments is problematic. The definition of what constitutes an institution varies across time and between different countries. Very broadly it would seem that most countries in western and northern Europe have about 4–6 per cent of their population aged 65 + resident in some form of institution. Data provided by Wall (1988) show that 10 per cent of those aged 65 + in Holland reside in an institution; this is the highest percentage in Europe. Parker (1987) indicates that in Australia 14 per cent of those aged 75 + live in an institution as compared with about 5 per cent in Britain. Given the limitations noted earlier we must, however, be cautious in drawing too many inferences from these kinds of data.

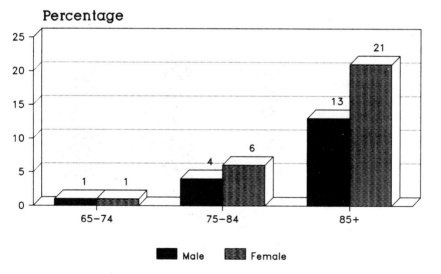

Fig. 2.3   Population aged 65 + resident in institutions in Great Britain, 1981
Source: Victor (1987).

FAMILY SIZE AND KIN RELATIONSHIPS

Patterns of family formation have changed significantly in Britain over the last century. These reflect changes in marriage rates, age at marriage, divorce and child bearing. For older people these changes influence the size of their kin networks by influencing the number of siblings they have and the numbers of children and grandchildren.

Age at first marriage has declined this century. The average age at first marriage is now about 23 years and the vast majority of the population, 90 per cent, has married by the age of 30 (CSO 1990). In addition family size has decreased. Between 1870 and 1930 average completed family size decreased from five or six children to three and has now stabilized at about two. In addition to this decrease in size child bearing is now concentrated into a much shorter period of a woman's life. In the middle of last century the average age at which a woman's family was completed was 39; it is now the late 20s (Finch 1989). This has resulted in siblings being born much closer together than in earlier time periods. The compression of child bearing has had important implications for the participation of women in the formal labour market. It also means that couples now spend a much larger part of the life cycle in the post child bearing phase.

One result of this compression of child bearing, combined with the decreased probability of children dying and increased life expectancy, is the creation of grandparenthood. It is now taken for granted that children will know their grandparents. This is a relatively new state of affairs which has resulted from the changes noted above.

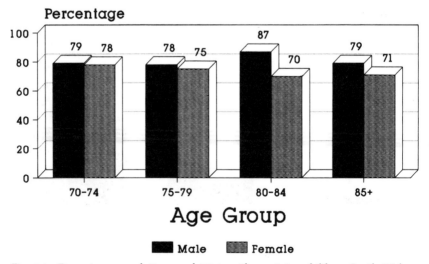

Fig. 2.4 Percentage population aged 70+ with surviving children, South Wales, 1980.
Source: Victor (1987), Table 10.1.

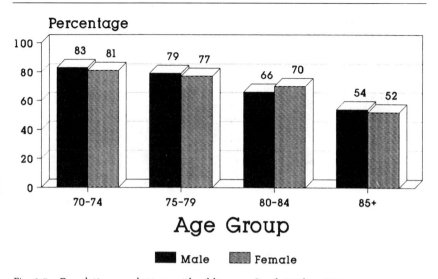

Fig. 2.5   Population aged 70 + with siblings in South Wales, 1980.
Source: Victor (1987), Table 10.2.

What are the consequences of these changes for the kin networks of the current generation of older people? The majority of those aged over 70 have both surviving siblings and children (see Figures 2.4 and 2.5). However the percentage with such family decreases with age. This decline is most notable with siblings; 80 per cent of those aged 70–74 report that they have brothers or sisters compared with about 50 per cent of those aged 85 +. However, these quantitative data tell us nothing about the quality or importance of the relationship. Indeed we know very little about contemporary kin relationships (Finch 1989) and can only speculate as to how increased rates of divorce and remarriage will affect family relationships.

SOCIAL CONTACT AND SOCIAL ISOLATION

One very potent image of later life is that of social isolation and loneliness. Invariably old age is portrayed by the image of an old lady living in obvious poverty and social neglect. How accurate is this representation? Are all older people socially isolated? Many social surveys of older people have focused upon issues concerning social contact and social isolation because of the potency of this image of isolation. This, of course, presents the methodological problem of how to measure social contact, social isolation and loneliness.

One way of tackling this problem is by enumerating the frequency with which an older person has contact with family, friends and neighbours. The General Household Survey provides extensive data concerning three main aspects of social contact: visits from friends/relatives; visits to friends/relatives

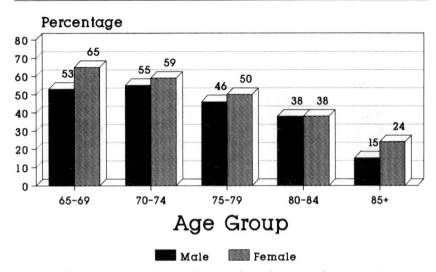

Fig. 2.6 Weekly visits to friends/relatives of population aged 65 + in Great Britain, 1985.
Source: OPCS (1988a), Table 12.24.

and contact with neighbours. Typically the survey asks if respondents have had contact with family/friends/neighbours on a scale ranging from daily to never. The available evidence shows that those aged 65 + maintain extensive weekly contact with both their family and friends. Only a small minority, about 5 per cent, are never visited by family/friends while 20 per cent report that they never go out to visit family/friends. Visits to friends/relatives decrease with age (Figure 2.6). This may reflect either the decreased mobility of older people or a decline in the number of friends and/or family available for visiting. However, with the exception of very elderly males (i.e. those aged 85 +), the percentage of those aged 65 + being visited at least weekly by their family or friends remains high, at about 70 per cent (Figure 2.7). Contact with neighbours, at least weekly, remains high (Figure 2.8).

This numerical analysis suggests that there is extensive social contact between older people and their families, friends and neighbours. What these empirical data cannot tell us is the quality of the interaction which has taken place. Such issues are most appropriately researched via more qualitative approaches.

Social isolation is a very nebulous concept to attempt to quantify. The simple quantitative approach described above suggests that very few older people are socially isolated; most have frequent contact with the wider social context. On a more subjective level social isolation may also refer to feelings of loneliness and concerns about the quality and quantity of social contacts. The main subjective component of social isolation examined by social researchers relates to loneliness. Typically researchers ask older people (or those from other age

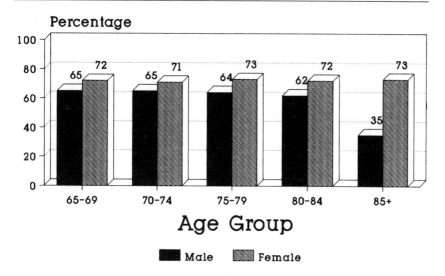

Fig. 2.7 Weekly visits from friends/family to population aged 65 + in Great Britain, 1985.
Source: OPCS (1988a), Table 12.25.

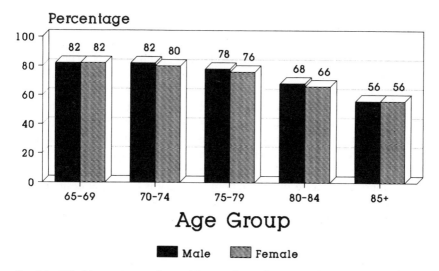

Fig. 2.8 Weekly contact with neighbours of population aged 65 + in Great Britain, 1985.
Source: OPCS (1988a), Table 12.29.

groups) to rate how often (if at all) they experience feelings of loneliness. Studies have consistently reported that the vast majority of older people, approximately 95 per cent, never feel lonely. Data from South Wales indicate that feelings of loneliness do seem to increase with age and are more common among women as compared with men. The percentage reporting that they sometimes felt lonely increased from 10 per cent of males and 16 per cent of females aged 70–74 to 18 per cent and 27 per cent respectively of those aged 85 + (Victor 1987). The percentage reporting that they always felt lonely showed little change with age.

The relationship between amount of social contact and feelings of loneliness is not linear. In South Wales 10 per cent of those who were classed as always alone, and therefore by implication as being socially isolated, reported that they often or always felt lonely.

It is clear that the vast majority of older people are neither socially isolated nor overwhelmed with feelings of loneliness. It is, however, difficult to conclude if older people are more (or less) socially isolated than younger members of society. Researchers have, very largely, identified loneliness as a problem of old age. Consequently these questions have rarely been put to younger members of society.

HOUSEHOLD STRUCTURE

The 1981 census enumerated 19,493,000 households in Great Britain living in the community. This, of course, excludes those people living in communal establishments such as prisons, hospitals or residential homes. The post-war period has also been characterized by very profound changes in family and household formation patterns. Indeed in the post-war period Great Britain has experienced a second demographic revolution relating to the structure and characteristics of the size of the households in which people live. There has been both an increase in the total number of households and a decrease in the average household size. This reflects very profound social changes in the number and type of independent households within contemporary Britain.

An important feature of contemporary society is the social desirability of creating and maintaining an independent household. Families sharing accommodation on a permanent basis is not now seen as socially desirable. This is reflected in the growth in the number of households and the decrease in household size. One index of this change is the growth of single person households. In 1961 12 per cent of all households in Great Britain consisted of one person as compared with 25 per cent in 1987 (Table 2.6). Single person pensioner households now represent 16 per cent of all households in Britain compared with 7 per cent in 1961 (CSO 1990). Single person households will represent an increasing proportion of all households in the future, perhaps as much as 31 per cent by 2001 if current trends persist (CSO 1990). However, the percentage of such householders who are pensioners is predicted to decrease

Table 2.6 Household composition in Great Britain (%), 1961, 1981 and 1987.

No of persons	1961	1981	1987
1	12	22	25
2	30	32	32
3	23	17	17
4+	45	29	26
mean size	3.09	2.71	2.55

Source: CSO (1989), Table 2.2.

from 60 per cent (1981) to 54 per cent (2001) (CSO 1990). Average household size has decreased from 3.09 in 1961 to 2.55 in 1987 and will continue to decline (Table 2.6).

Similar trends are observable in mainland Europe. For example, in 1981 31 per cent of households in the Federal Republic of Germany and 29 per cent in Denmark consisted of a single person (CSO 1989).

Against this background of significant changes in household formation patterns it is hardly surprising that there has been an increase in the proportion and number of older people living alone (Figure 2.9). The percentage of people aged 65 and over living alone has increased from 10 per cent in 1945 to 36 per cent in 1985, while the percentage of those living with others has decreased from 60 per cent to 20 per cent over the same period. These changes reflect a variety of social factors, including the decrease in the age of marriage, a

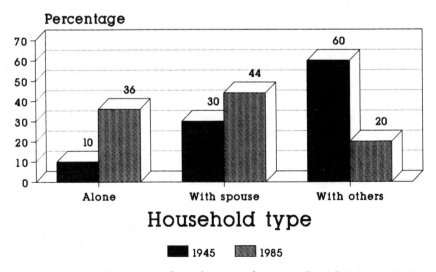

Fig. 2.9 Household structure of population aged 65 + in Great Britain, 1945–85. *Source:* Dale *et al.* (1987), Table 1.

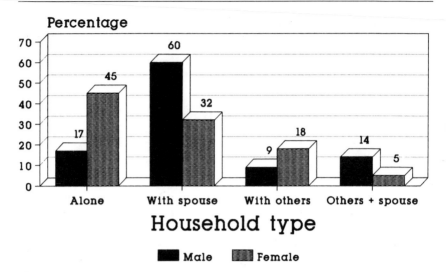

Fig. 2.10 Household structure by sex of population aged 65 + in Great Britain, 1985.
Source: Wall (1988).

decrease in the average age at which the last child is born combined with a closer spacing of children. These trends, allied with the increased life expectancy of older people, have combined with the result that children are increasingly likely to have left the parental home to establish an independent household before the death of their parents. This results in a shortening of the average duration of time in which families live as a nuclear group and an increase in the phase of the life cycle in which the couple live alone post-child rearing – the empty nest phase. These changes also reflect the increased ability of older people to financially maintain their own households after the children have left home and a very strong social desire by all age groups to be independent.

At all ages older women are more likely to be living alone than their male contemporaries (Figure 2.10). Almost half of women aged 65 + (45 per cent) live alone compared with 17 per cent of males. As would be expected from the evidence about marital status presented earlier more men (60 per cent) live with their spouses than do women (32 per cent). The large concentration of older people living by themselves has tended to divert attention away from the often complex household structures in which older people live. Dale et al. (1987) report that a 25-category classification system was required to fully represent the variety of types of household structure in which older people in Great Britain lived.

Despite the availability of statistics describing societal level changes in household formation which have influenced the type of household in which older people live, this still remains the subject of considerable mythology. As Finch (1989) describes, it is commonly asserted that this century has seen the demise of the extended family structure which is commonly assumed to have been the norm at previous points in time. Laslett (1972) has demonstrated unambiguously that three generation or extended households were not the norm in pre-industrial times for the simple reason that comparatively few older people were found in the population before the later part of this century. Furthermore, Finch (1989) suggests that much co-residence between relatives was driven by economic imperatives and was often for a temporary period only. We should also not make the rather simplistic assumption that co-residence implies a strong bond between relatives. Nor does the setting up of separate households necessarily imply a weakening of social and caring relationships.

GEOGRAPHICAL DISTRIBUTION

Within Britain, and other countries, older people are not equally geographically distributed. This has important social and health policy implications as planning, at both national and local levels, must take this imbalance into account. The main concentrations of older people in Britain are on the south coast, in subsidiary retirement areas such as the north-east and north Wales coast and within inner city areas, especially in the north and north-west. Several factors account for this distribution: the ageing of populations *in situ*; out-migration of the young and in-migration of older people. The relationship between these factors in determining the spatial distribution of the elderly is unknown and probably varies historically. However, most of the current distribution is probably accounted for by the ageing of local populations with migration being of secondary importance. Evidence for this is provided by the relatively low rates of geographical mobility in Britain as compared with other countries. Evidence for the importance of ageing *in situ* can be seen from the ring of 'ageing' suburbs of both private and public sector housing which surround many of the large cities in Britain.

ETHNICITY

Issues regarding the ethnic minority dimensions of ageing are only now beginning to be addressed in Britain. At the 1981 census people of pensionable age represented less than 4 per cent of all households with a head drawn from the New Commonwealth (Asia, the Indian subcontinent and Pakistan).

A feature of British society in the next 25 years will be the ageing of the ethnic minority communities who came to the country in the 1960s to provide labour (Figure 2.11). We know very little about how the experience of ageing will vary between those who came to this country as economic migrants and the indigenous population. We have little hard information about how ageing

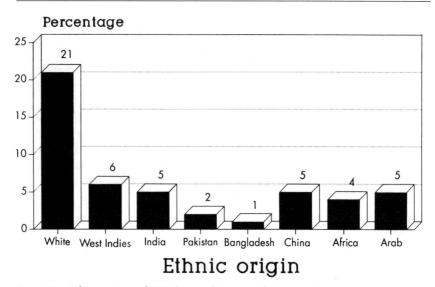

Fig. 2.11 Ethnic origin of British population aged 60+, 1985–87.
Source: CSO (1989), Table 1.5.

affects minority communities. However, we have a number of potent stereotypes about the 'more caring' nature of minority communities and their reluctance to use formal services to provide care traditionally provided by the family in their country of origin. The accuracy of these images remains unproven. There is much work to be done in enumerating the real needs of minority elders for services and to develop services which respond to the cultural needs of these communities.

The social circumstances of older people

Several aspects of the social circumstances of older people are important when discussing their ability to pay for the care they require. These are economic activity, financial situation and housing type and quality.

ECONOMIC ACTIVITY

Economic activity rates are low among those of pensionable age. Data from the 1981 census indicates that 7 per cent of women aged 65–69 and 17 per cent of men were defined as economically active (see Figures 2.12, 2.13). These low rates of economic activity reflect the requirement to have formally retired from paid work in order to receive the state retirement pension in Britain.

Since 1951 there has been a significant decrease in the labour force participation of older male workers. During the 30 years from 1951 to 1981 the proportion of males aged 60–64 who were defined as economically active decreased from 87.5 per cent to 74.6 (Figure 2.12). Johnson (1988) observes that this decrease is not a new phenomenon but is a continuation of trends which have their origin in the last century. However, the pace of decline has quickened in the post-war period. Similar trends may be observed in most western industrial societies.

The factors used to explain the decreased labour market participation of older men may be classified into three groups: health, economic and structural. Poor health and disability are both consistently associated with early exit from the labour market. Both Parker (1980) and Walker (1985) have shown that ill health is an important factor in the decision to take early retirement. However, the validity of these findings is challengeable as respondents may feel encouraged to give socially acceptable reasons for early retirement such as ill health rather than factors such as self-interest. Economic variables such as the demand for labour and the state of the economy are obviously important in the retirement decision. Phillipson (1982) has argued that older workers form a 'reserve' army of labour which can be recruited in times of labour shortage and discarded during periods of depression. The third set of factors are structural and include the availability of private pensions and social security income entitlements. Johnson (1988) investigated the interrelationships between these sets of factors and concluded that structural reasons have become increasingly important in the early retirement decision. However, he also concludes that the precise relationship between these influences upon the decision to retire from work early probably varies between different sectors of the economy.

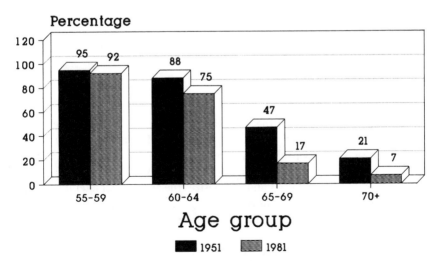

Fig. 2.12 Economic activity of males in Great Britain, 1951–81.
Source: Falkingham (1989).

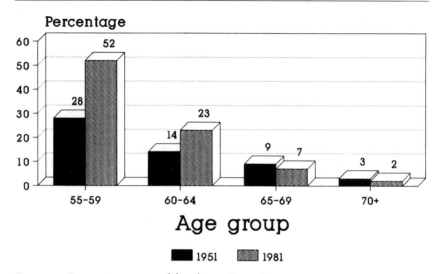

Fig. 2.13 Economic activity of females in Great Britain, 1951–81.
Source: Falkingham (1989).

For women the picture is more complex. The post-war period has seen an increase in labour force participation (see Figure 2.13). For women aged 55–59 the percentage classified as economically active increased from 28 per cent in 1951 to 52 per cent in 1981. As yet there has been little research considering early retirement among women and its social meaning and impact. At a very superficial level it has been suggested that retirement is not problematic for women because of the importance of their 'other' social roles. It remains to be seen if this impressionistic statement is correct or whether it will apply to future generations of elderly women who have been active in the labour market for most of their adult life.

FINANCIAL SITUATION

Two contrasting images of the financial and living standards of older people may be identified. The first casts older people as being almost inevitably poor and this draws a causal relationship between income and later life. This is a perspective with a long historical pedigree. A more recent image is diametrically opposed to this and emphasizes the affluence of later life. It is this perspective which has generated the image of the woopies (well off older people), opals (older people with affluent lifestyles) and the jolies (jet setting oldies with loads of loot).

Older people who remain active in the formal labour market will be in receipt of earnings from employment. Those not gainfully employed are dependent upon two main sources for their income: pensions and savings. Pensions may be received from two main sources: the state and previous employers. First, there is the state retirement pension. This is known colloquially as the old age pension and is payable at a flat rate to all those who have finally retired from the labour market provided they have the appropriate national insurance contributions. For those older people with an income below a defined level additional pensions are payable. Up to April 1988 this was known as supplementary pension and was the arm of the supplementary benefit system catering for older people. Since April 1988 this has been replaced by income support. Older people may also be in receipt of a pension from a previous employer (an occupational pension). Furthermore, older people may have savings or investments which will yield income. This is termed unearned income. Support from relatives may also be received but it is difficult to quantify this source of income and it is excluded from the analysis which follows.

Since the immediate post-war period older people have become more reliant upon the state for their income (Figure 2.14). In 1951 42 per cent of pensioners' income derived from the state compared with 60 per cent in 1984/85. Over the same period the percentage derived from earnings has decreased from 27 per cent to 9 per cent. The state is the most important single source of income for the older age groups. The levels at which state pensions are paid is, therefore, crucial to the standard of living of older people.

International comparative studies of the income levels of specific social groups such as the elderly remain rare because of the difficulties involved in making comparisons between societies with widely differing responses to the issue of income maintenance in later life. These problems are compounded by

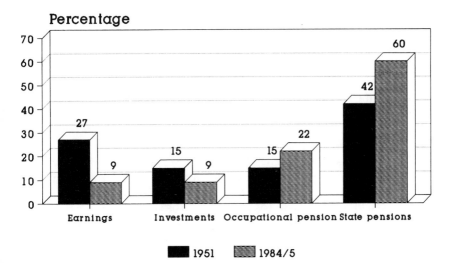

Fig. 2.14   Sources of income for pensioners in Great Britain, 1951 and 1984/85.
Source: OECD (1988).

differences in absolute and relative levels of income between societies. At this macro level of analysis it has been demonstrated that older people in Britain experience an income level relative to other members of society which is considerably below that enjoyed by their counterparts in Europe and North America (Hedstrom and Ringen 1987). These authors indicate that the incomes of the 65–74 age group in Britain are 76 per cent of the population average compared with 94 per cent for the other six European and North American countries included within their study. Thus Hedstrom and Ringen (1987, p. 238) state that 'with the exception of Britain, the standard of living of elderly families is not far behind the national average'. At the international level of analysis it seems that the elderly in Britain fare much worse than their European colleagues. However, the limitations of these data must be borne in mind, especially the fact that they are limited to a single point in time.

These authors also examined the distribution of income within the elderly populations of the countries studied. This exercise revealed that the elderly in Britain were characterized by less income inequality than their European counterparts. This paradox is explained by the fact that in Britain the vast majority of older people are poor and there is therefore less difference in income levels between the group. This is in direct contrast to the European studies where there are much greater variations within the elderly population in terms of income levels.

There is a substantial body of research comparing the income of the retired population in Britain with those below retirement age. Optimistic statements from government sources suggest that the real incomes of the retired are increasing and that this group is improving its economic position with regard to the rest of society.

Fiegehen (1986) reports that the share of total disposable personal income (TDPI) attributable to pensioners has increased from 7 per cent in 1951 to 15 per cent in 1984/85. During this period the percentage of retired people within the population increased from 13 per cent to 18 per cent. The source of the increased disposable income of older people is attributed to two factors: the growth of the pensionable population and increased affluence of older people. This increase in TDPI may simply reflect the fact that pensioners start from a very low base. It also calls into question what percentage of TDPI pensioners ought to represent.

The poverty statistics are cited as further support for the view that the elderly are becoming better off in relation to the rest of society. In 1950 pensioners constituted 70 per cent of those claiming supplementary benefit compared with 59 per cent in 1984/85 (DHSS 1984). However, this change has been brought about almost entirely by the increase in the long-term unemployed rather than an increase in the living standards of older people in the lowest income groups; it is not the result of a vast increase in the incomes of older people. Rather it reflects the creation of an even poorer group, the long-term unemployed, who have very low incomes.

It seems that older people in Britain are better off than some other groups dependent upon welfare for their source of income; but they have not improved their situation with regard to those in employment. The prevalence of poverty among this group remains very high, although we should not neglect the fact that there are a minority of affluent elderly. Overall approximately 25 per cent of those aged 65 + have an income at or below supplementary benefit rates and a further 44 per cent live on the margins of poverty, i.e. they have an income within 40 per cent of the poverty level (Victor 1989a). Within the elderly population, it is the very old (i.e. those aged over 80), women, those living alone, those from manual occupations and the disabled who are most at risk of experiencing poverty in later life (Victor 1989a).

HOUSING CIRCUMSTANCES

The population aged 65 + is often characterized as being income poor but asset rich. This refers to the fact that, as Figure 2.15 shows, 50 per cent of those aged 65 + are home owners. Unlike younger age groups those over retirement age are usually actual home owners as opposed to holding a mortgage. Overall about 35–40 per cent of those aged 65 + rent accommodation from the local authority (public sector housing), with the remainder renting from a private landlord. The percentage classed as home owners is projected to increase to 60 per cent by the year 2000. Young elderly will illustrate a higher rate of home ownership than the older elderly. One reason for the interest in rates of home ownership among the older age groups is the potential of realizing the asset and

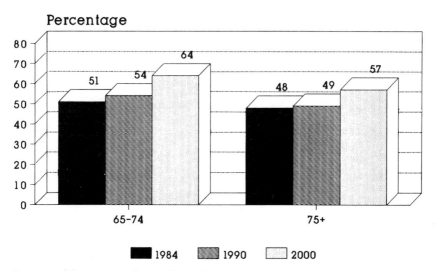

Fig. 2.15 Home ownership in Great Britain, 1984–2000.
Source: Laing and Propper (1990), Table 3.10.

using it to pay for care. Such schemes neglect the importance of inheritance, the desire by older people to leave something to their children or grandchildren. The widespread promotion of such asset liberating schemes would, of course, do nothing for those without a house to sell or realize the capital value of.

Conclusion

There is a trend throughout the countries of western Europe and North America for the ageing of the population. These trends look set to continue into the early decades of the next millennium. However, it is not yet possible to predict with any certainty what proportion of the population the older age groups will represent as future fertility remains the subject of considerable speculation. It seems likely that the trend towards the establishment of separate households will continue, and this will result in more older people living alone or with their spouses. Several features of the older age groups which are currently taken for granted, including the predominance of women and the stereotype of the elderly spinster, in part reflect cohort effects; future generations are unlikely to display these trends to the same degree. Thus predicting the future health and social care needs of the older age groups, as indicated by demographic factors, is largely speculative.

3 PHYSICAL HEALTH: PATTERNS OF MORTALITY

The high profile of biological theories and perspectives in gerontology have resulted in a perceived general association between age and (ill) health. To be old is to be, of necessity, unhealthy. This image of old age is not new. De Beauvoir (1985 p. 104) quotes the rather gloomy view of old age written by the Egyptian poet Ptah-hotep in 2500 BC

> How hard and painful are the last days of an aged man! He grows weaker every day; his eyes become dim, his ears deaf; his strength fades; his heart knows peace no longer; his mouth falls silent and speaks no word. The power of his mind lessens and today he cannot remember what yesterday was like. All his bones hurt. Those things which not long ago were done with pleasure are painful now; and taste vanishes. Old age is the worst of misfortune that can afflict a man. His nose is blocked, and he can smell nothing any more.

From a health policy perspective the scenario depicted is that the increasing numbers of older people described earlier will lead to the population of the western industrial nations being infirm, demented and disease ridden with an insatiable demand for health and social care. The greying of nations is presented as an inescapable world wide pandemic from which there is no escape. Furthermore, old age is perceived by both lay people and professional workers alike as a cause of ill health. Blaxter (1983) in her study of women's thoughts on health and the cause of disease clearly identifies an acceptance of poor health as an attribute of normal ageing. Conversely youth is depicted as a time of vitality and good health. These stereotypes form the context within which to attempt to consider the health of older people and the relationship between health and ageing and variations in health status within the older age groups, using a variety of different measures including mortality, morbidity and disability. Before presenting the empirical data concerning health status, the thesis developed by Fries concerning future patterns of mortality and morbidity in later life is described.

Health in later life: the thesis of Fries

The tone of the debate about the health implications has been overwhelmingly negative. One of the most interesting theoretical propositions about ageing and health status has been proposed by Fries (1980) in an article in the *New England Journal of Medicine* and subsequently developed in more detail (Fries and Crapo 1981). Fries outlined a twin set of ideas about the health of older people termed the 'rectangularisation of mortality' and 'compression of morbidity' based upon his observations, as a practising clinician, of North American society. Each of these ideas is considered separately although the two processes are inter-related.

The first part of the argument relates to the rather alarmingly titled concept of 'rectangularisation of mortality'. This term relates to the effect upon natural lifespan of a decrease in premature mortality. Fries made the assumption that the natural lifespan of the human species is of fixed duration; in his work he takes this as 85 years. As premature mortality decreases, he argues, more people will live to the limits of this natural lifespan. This will greatly increase mortality at the end of the natural lifespan creating an almost rectangular pattern of mortality (see Figure 3.1).

Fries argued that the elimination of much premature mortality would result in the creation of 'natural death'. By this he meant that death would result from the body 'wearing out' at the end of the natural lifecourse rather than early death resulting from disease or trauma.

The second element of Fries's argument relates to the 'compression of morbidity'. He indicates that, with the control of premature mortality largely

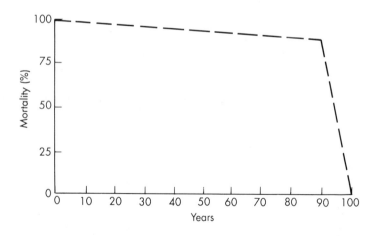

Fig. 3.1 The rectangularization of mortality.
Source: After Fries (1980).

the result of reducing mortality from infectious diseases, the pattern of population morbidity will be dominated by chronic diseases. If the onset of such diseases can be delayed then morbidity will be compressed into the final years of life. He argues that more people will live to the full extent of their lifespans and that the onset of disability will be squeezed into the last phase of life. This delay in the onset of chronic disease would increase the number of disability free years in old age which the average person would experience. This rather optimistic view would, therefore, suggest that an increase in the elderly population need not be problematic in health care terms as the population might not display as much morbidity as current cohorts.

These propositions have been hotly debated and a variety of different responses were soon forthcoming (see Bury 1988). Fries's argument is dependent upon the notion of a fixed human lifespan. He felt that the idea that the human lifespan could continue to increase was biologically implausible. Several authors have argued that there is no evidence to support this proposition (Manton 1982; Schneider and Brody 1983). Neither do they support the view that mortality in late life is due to the body 'wearing out', as Fries asserts, rather than to specific and clinically identifiable disease states. This debate as to whether the human lifespan is indeed finite remains unresolved. It has also been suggested that the ideas proposed by Fries rest upon an assumption that mortality rates in later life have reached a plateau and will not show further changes. In both Britain and the United States late age mortality rates have decreased markedly in the post-war period (see below). These changes in mortality, especially among the old elderly, suggest that we have not reached the maximum human lifespan.

There are also problems with the compression of morbidity thesis, most notably the lack of any clear and rigorous evidence of decreases in morbidity and the non-availability of measures of morbidity with which to test his proposition. Bury (1988) also points out that the argument concerning decreasing mortality and morbidity rates is contaminated by cohort effects and influences. Fries argues that preventive activities can result in the delayed onset of morbidity and chronic disease. Again, there is remarkably little evidence to support (or indeed refute) the argument that an 'active and healthy lifestyle' can delay the onset of disease and disability in later life.

The debate about the validity of these twin propositions continues. Bury (1988) provides some interesting ideas about how the debate can be moved forward by designing research projects which examine ageing from a longitudinal perspective. He also illustrates how the debate has become obscured by competing ideological perspectives about the value of prevention in influencing the onset of disease and disability in later life. The status of Fries's ideas remains that of interesting speculation. However, they have been of considerable value in that they have challenged the assumptions of many gerontologists and policy makers and forced a closer examination of our knowledge about health and ageing in later life.

Mortality

In the United Kingdom the 1836 Births and Deaths Registration Act provides the framework for the current system of death registration. All deaths must be notified with the Registrar of Births, Deaths and Marriages. A death certificate is completed by the certifying doctor and gives details of the disease which resulted in death, and any underlying conditions. The certificate also includes details of the name, sex, final occupation and place of residence of the deceased person. The information provided on the death certificate provides the basis of mortality data which are eventually published and analysed by researchers and social commentators. The death certificates are collated and analysed by the Office of Population Censuses and Surveys (OPCS). The main cause of death is classified using the international classification of diseases (ICD). These data are then made available in a variety of different forms.

There are practical problems with the use of mortality data. These include considerations of the completeness of the system's coverage and the delay in making the data available. There is generally a two-year time lag in the information being made available due to the large size and complexity of the data set. This may not matter with mortality data, where it seems unlikely that there would be very rapid transformation in the main causes of death. More important are questions concerning the accuracy of the identification of the cause of death, especially for older people.

Mortality data are, therefore, readily available in Britain. Consequently mortality is the oldest and most widely used index of health status. Indeed, debates about changes in health status are dominated by the use of traditional health indices such as mortality. Evidence to support (or refute) variations in health status within and between populations is typically presented in terms of differences in death rates. The use of mortality data to describe the health status of the population is based upon the assumption that mortality is a good proxy measure of the amount and main causes of morbidity within the population.

In 1987 there were 566,994 deaths certified in England and Wales (OPCS 1989b). The majority of these deaths, 450,630 (79 per cent) were of people aged 65 and over (see Table 3.1). Deaths before the age of 65, so-called premature deaths, are comparatively rare. One general index calculated from death and population information is the crude death rate. This simply expresses the total number of deaths per 1000 total population. The crude death rate in England and Wales in 1987 was 11.4 per 1000 for males and 11.1 per 1000 for females.

PATTERNS OF MORTALITY

A number of more specific indices may be calculated from aggregate death and population data. When looking at changes over time (or making comparisons between areas) one way of overcoming differences in overall population structure is via the calculation of age and sex specific mortality rates. The overall

Table 3.1   Age and sex specific deaths in England and Wales, 1987.

Age	Rate per million		Total deaths	
	M	F	M	F
Under 1	5238	4009	3637	2635
1–4	440	392	578	489
5–14	225	161	713	483
15–24	781	296	3200	1164
25–34	884	476	3218	1708
35–44	1671	1125	5823	3897
45–54	5007	3225	13678	8774
55–64	15973	9135	41267	25000
65–74	41225	22753	82021	56858
75–84	96301	60065	94060	103354
85 +	191548	158560	31882	82455
Total	10654	10304	280177	286817

Source: OPCS (1989b), Tables 3 and B.

distribution of mortality rates within the population shows a J-shaped distribution. Mortality is relatively high in the first year of life and then decreases during childhood (see Table 3.1). From the age of 15 years mortality rates then start to increase.

For the population aged 65 two main trends are evident. First, the mortality rate increases with age from 41.2 per 1000 for males aged 65–74 to 191.5 per 1000 for men aged 85 + (Table 3.1). Similar age-related increases are observed for women. Second, at each age mortality rates are lower for women as compared with men (this is considered in more detail below). This gender difference in mortality is not specific to later life but is a pattern which is observable at all ages (see Table 3.1).

GENDER DIFFERENCES IN MORTALITY

At all ages for those aged 65 + female death rates are substantially lower than those for males. This male–female difference in mortality was not very marked at the start of the century but has now emerged strongly. In the early decades of last century gender differences in late life mortality were very small. For example, the excess male mortality was 10 per cent for those aged 65–74 and 5 per cent for those aged 85 +. This contrasts with the position for 1981–85 where in the 65–74 age group men have a mortality rate 87 per cent above their female counterparts (see Table 3.2). Even in the over-85 age group males have mortality rates 25 per cent above those for women.

There are two main hypotheses for male–female differences in mortality: biological/genetic and social/environmental factors. Verbrugge (1989) considers that only 10 per cent of the gender difference in late-age mortality is due

Table 3.2   Male–female mortality ratios in England and Wales.

	65–74	75–84	85+	*All ages*
1841–45	1.10	1.09	1.05	1.02
1901–05	1.19	1.14	1.10	1.06
1961–65	1.81	1.45	1.22	1.04
1971–75	1.93	1.54	1.25	1.03
1981–85	1.87	1.60	1.25	1.04

Source: Own calculations from OPCS (1989a).

Table 3.3   Mortality rates per 1000 by sex and age in four countries.

	Year	65–74 Male	Female	Ratio	75+ Male	Female	Ratio
Australia	1983	38.2	19.7	1.93	106.1	77.3	1.37
England–Wales	1982	45.8	24.3	1.88	121.0	89.6	1.35
Japan	1984	29.3	15.9	1.84	96.9	71.3	1.35
USA	1982	39.3	20.9	1.88	101.9	72.9	1.39

Source: Kalache *et al.* (1988), Figure 2.

to biological or intrinsic factors and 90 per cent is a result of differences in social variables such as smoking behaviour; Waldron (1976) suggests that 75 per cent of the difference is attributable to behavioural factors. Gee and Veevers (1983) offer a more sophisticated hypothesis. They propose that the relationship between biological and social factors in explaining gender differences in mortality may vary over the lifecourse. They suggest that social and environmental factors are most important in the early phases of life with biological/genetic factors more important in later life. This implies that social and behavioural factors explain the failure of men to survive to later life but biological factors then maintain the mortality advantage of women in later life.

INTERNATIONAL VARIATIONS IN LATE-AGE MORTALITY

There are substantial differences in mortality rates among older people in developed countries (Table 3.3). The late-age mortality rates prevalent in Japan are considerably better than in the other three comparison countries. For example, Japanese mortality rates for the 65–74 age group are only 60 per cent of those prevalent in Great Britain. For those aged 75 + mortality rates in Japan are 20 per cent lower than those recorded for Great Britain. This offers the prospect of further room for improvement in late-age mortality in most developed countries. Excess male mortality appears constant across the four very different countries included in the table.

Table 3.4   Deaths by underlying cause in England and Wales, 1987.

ISD 9 code	ICD 9 chapter heading	Total deaths M	F	Deaths aged 65 + M	F
001–139	Infectious and parasitic diseases	1204	1171	653	779
140–239	Neoplasms	74325	68126	53879	48487
240–279	Endocrine diseases	4213	5597	3008	4809
280–289	Blood diseases	900	1423	729	1263
290–319	Mental disorders	4140	8297	3662	5806
320–389	Nervous diseases	5251	5702	3726	4457
390–459	Circulatory diseases	132599	138462	103011	127190
460–519	Respiratory diseases	29712	27363	26059	25006
520–579	Digestive diseases	7414	10255	5416	8720
580–629	Genito-urinary	3463	4233	3157	3937
639–679	Pregnancy and childbirth	—	46	—	—
680–709	Skin	176	558	151	528
710–739	Musculo-skeletal	1222	3970	1055	3642
740–759	Congenital anomalies	936	858	150	172
760–779	Perinatal conditions	122	76	—	—
780–799	Ill-defined conditions	1504	2405	521	1778
800–999	Accidents and violence	10991	6832	2785	3851
Total		280177	286817	207963	242667

Source: OPCS (1989b), Tables C and 2.

THE MAJOR CAUSES OF DEATH IN THE UNITED KINGDOM

What are the main causes of death? Under the system of death registration functioning in the United Kingdom the cause of death must be described on the death certificate. The returns on individual certificates are coded using the international classification of diseases, and aggregate data about the main causes of mortality in the population are published. Given the complexity of this task there is always a time lag in the publication of mortality by cause of death data.

Although rates of mortality differ between men and women the main causes of mortality do not. Examined in very broad terms for both men and women the two largest single causes of death are circulatory diseases (e.g. heart disease, stroke, etc.) and cancers of all sites (see Table 3.4). This pattern of mortality has remained approximately constant over the post-war period. Within each of the broad ICD chapters the vast majority of deaths are of older people (Table 3.4).

Causes of mortality in later life

Does the pattern of mortality change with increasing age? The four main causes of mortality in later life are heart disease, cancers, respiratory diseases,

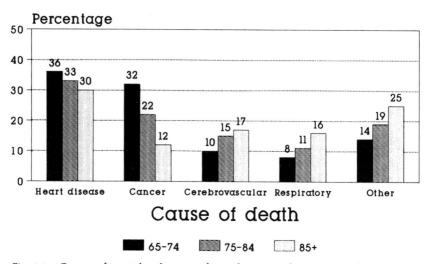

Fig. 3.2   Causes of mortality by age of population aged 65 + in England and Wales, 1987.
Source: OPCS (1989b).

cerebrovascular disease (stroke). These diseases account for 71 per cent of deaths in those aged 65 +. With increasing age the percentage of deaths attributable to heart disease and cancer decreases, while that for cerebrovascular disease (stroke) and respiratory diseases increases (Figure 3.2).

People aged 65 + account for 72 per cent of all cancer deaths in England and Wales (see Table 3.5). The broad ICD chapter heading of cancers encompasses a whole variety of different types and sites of cancers. However, some sites of cancer are much more common than others. For both women and men the largest source of cancer mortality is that relating to the digestive organs (e.g. stomach, etc.). This accounts for about 30 per cent of all deaths from cancer; the second largest source of cancer mortality is lung cancer for men (33 per cent of all deaths) and breast cancer for women (20 per cent) of all cancer deaths. Lung cancer accounts for 15 per cent of female cancer deaths.

All of these sources of cancer mortality include an element of preventability. This is at its most extreme for lung cancer, which is an almost entirely avoidable cause of death (i.e. it is strongly associated with smoking). For the older age groups there is a distinct gender difference in the importance of lung cancer as a cause of death. For older men it accounts for between 20–40 per cent of cancer deaths. In contrast lung cancer is a much less important cause of death for older women. This reflects the comparative rarity of smoking among very elderly women (see Chapter 6). No doubt this pattern of mortality will be influenced by the ageing of generations where a large percentage of women have smoked.

For women of all ages breast cancer and cancer of the cervix account for 18 per cent of cancer deaths. Both types of cancer are now subject to national

Table 3.5 Cancer deaths of population aged 65 + in England and Wales, 1987.

Site	65–74 years				75–84 years				85+ years				All ages			
	M n	%	F n	%	M n	%	F n	%	M n	%	F n	%	M n	%	F n	%
Digestive organs	7319	29	5046	27	6295	29	7051	34	1552	24	3577	39	21452	29	19343	28
Lung, trachea and bronchus	9723	38	3759	20	7363	32	2856	14	1157	22	731	8	24830	33	10308	15
Cervix	—	—	476	3	—	—	295	1	—	—	104	1	—	—	1903	3
Breast	—	—	3376	18	—	—	3326	16	—	—	1641	18	—	—	13751	20
All	25566	—	18855	—	23032	—	20498	—	5281	—	9134	—	74325	—	68126	—

Source: OPCS (1989b), Table 2.

screening programmes as early detection may prevent these cancers being fatal. However, both schemes only screen women up to the age of 65 years although those aged 65 + represent 60 per cent of all breast cancer deaths and 46 per cent of cervical cancer deaths. It is not clear why the age of 65 was taken as the cut-off point for these screening programmes. For cervical cancer it has been suggested that physiological reasons make it more difficult to take good smears from older women. However, the reasons for selecting these cut-off points has not been the subject of debate. For both diseases women outside the screening programme account for the majority of deaths. As we shall see in a later section a woman aged 65 can expect to live for almost another 20 years. Fletcher (1990) has argued for the extension of cervical screening after the age of 65 years but as yet there has been no similar argument for breast cancer screening.

Heart disease and stroke are very prevalent among the older age groups. In England and Wales those aged 65 + represent the majority of deaths from all forms of heart disease and strokes. The stereotype of the coronary heart disease patient is that of a middle-aged man. Mortality data indicate that only a minority of such deaths occur in 'the executive male'. Both forms of mortality death rates increase progressively with age and this reflects the pattern of incidence described by community studies. Again, these diseases can be reduced by preventive activity as both are strongly linked to smoking behaviour and, to a lesser degree, to other lifestyle factors such as diet and exercise.

CHANGES IN MORTALITY

How have mortality rates changed over time? In Britain death registration and population data are available from the 1840s onwards. Overall the crude death rate has decreased markedly in Britain over this century. In 1901–04 the male crude death rate was 17.0 per 1000; for women it was 15.0 per 1000 (see Table 3.6). Making comparisons of crude death rates across time or between populations is problematic as the rate is obviously influenced by the age composition of populations: a population with a large component of older people will illustrate a higher crude death rate than a population of the same size including a lot of younger people. To overcome such problems comparisons are usually made via the calculation of standardized mortality ratios (SMRs). Taking the period 1950–52 as the standard, the SMR for England and Wales has decreased from 249 (1901–04) to 75 (1980–84) (OPCS 1989a). As measured by the mortality index, the health status of the population has improved markedly over the last century and a half.

During the post-war period the crude mortality rate for England and Wales has showed little change (see Table 3.6). However, over this period there has been a substantial improvement in late age (i.e. 65 +) mortality in Britain (Table 3.6). Since 1961 there has been a 19 per cent decrease in the mortality rates for males aged 65–74. The largest percentage decrease in mortality during these

Table 3.6 Mortality rates in England and Wales.

| | 65–74 | | 75–84 | | 85+ | | All ages | |
	M	F	M	F	M	F	M	F
1841–45	65.5	59.1	143.7	131.8	305.1	288.6	22.1	20.6
1901–05	65.3	54.8	137.6	119.9	274.6	249.4	17.0	15.0
1961–65	54.0	29.8	121.3	83.6	253.2	206.7	12.4	11.2
1971–75	51.1	26.4	115.1	74.5	237.1	188.9	12.3	11.4
1981–85	45.2	24.1	103.5	64.4	220.8	175.9	11.9	11.4
% change								
1961–85	−19	−24	−17	−30	−15	−18	−4	+2

Rate per 1000 population

Source: OPCS (1989a), Table 2.

three decades is shown by women aged 75–84. These trends are not unique to Britain and may be observed in various countries. For example, in the United States there was a 16 per cent decline in mortality rates among males aged 85 + and 36 per cent among females of the same age during the period 1965–85 (Verbrugge 1989). The reasons for these declines in late-age mortality are not well understood but probably reflect a variety of factors including better health care and improvements in nutrition and other aspects of living conditions as well as improvements in the availability and quality of medical care.

Have these overall changes in mortality been reflected equally in the different causes of death? This simple question is rather less easy to answer. The evaluation of changes in disease specific mortality rates over time is problematic because of changes in classification procedures and death certification practices.

For the North American white population aged 65 + there have been significant decreases in mortality from stroke and ischaemic heart disease. Between 1968 and 1976 mortality from ischaemic heart disease in women aged 85 + decreased by 21 per cent and by 17 per cent for males (Verbrugge 1989). Similar decreases in heart disease mortality and stroke mortality have been observed in a variety of different countries (Smith and Jacobson 1988), although the decreases observed in the United Kingdom have been less dramatic than those recorded in some other countries.

The reduction of mortality from both stroke and ischaemic heart disease are characteristic of much of the developed world. However, the decreases observed in Britain are smaller than those recorded in other countries. For example, Japan recorded decreases in overall stroke mortality for both men and women of about 50 per cent between 1972 and 1982; in England and Wales the decrease was about 35 per cent over the same period (Smith and Jacobson 1988). Satisfactory explanations for these reductions in mortality from circulatory diseases have not yet been arrived at and may reflect a change in the disease, improved medical care or changes in lifestyle habits.

Table 3.7   Changes in mortality 1951–55 to 1980–84 in England and Wales.

	\% change									
	60–64		65–69		70–74		75–79		80–84	
	M	F	M	F	M	F	M	F	M	F
Ischaemic heart	+15	+8	+6	−16	−15	−27	−21	−38	−34	−47
Bronchitis	−62	−26	−50	−38	−30	−49	−6	−60	+11	−60
Lung cancer	+16	+327	+54	+350	+240	+350	+368	+262	+899	+329

Source: Alderson and Ashwood (1985), Table 3.

Data from Alderson and Ashwood (1985) examining changes in cause specific late-age mortality between 1950–54 and 1980–84 confirm the general patterns outlined above. There have also between significant decreases in late-age mortality from ischaemic heart disease and bronchitis (Table 3.7). However, mortality from lung cancer increased significantly over this period. This reflects the ageing of cohorts where smoking had been a more prevalent lifestyle habit. This trend gives considerable cause for concern as lung cancer is an almost totally avoidable source of mortality.

WHO (1988) provide statistics for the 65–74 age group for the United Kingdom for the same time period as Alderson and Ashwood (1985). These data show that for the 65–74 age group mortality from stroke decreased by 42 per cent for males and 50 per cent for females. Significant decreases in mortality from heart disease and respiratory diseases are also observable from these data. However, overall cancer mortality increased by 24 per cent and 9 per cent respectively for men and women and lung cancer mortality has approximately doubled. For women mortality from breast cancer increased by 17 per cent. Indeed, Alderson (1988) observes that age-specific mortality rates for breast cancer have remained essentially static this century and to date there is little evidence that early detection and treatment of this disease is having much effect.

EXPECTATION OF LIFE

Changes in mortality have had an effect upon life expectancy – the age to which the average person can expect to live. Life expectancy is usually calculated from birth but may be computed for any age. In 1906 life expectancy at birth for a male in Britain was 48 years and 51 years for a female; in 1985 the average expectation of life at birth was 71 and 77 years respectively (see Figure 3.3). The average child born in Britain can expect to live, on average, 23 years more than its counterparts born at the turn of the century. Expectation of life at age 65 has increased less dramatically over this century; 2.4 years for men and 5.3 years for women. Even so, a 65-year-old male can expect to live for another 13.2 years and a female of the same age for 17.2 years.

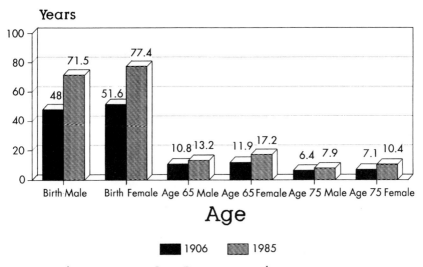

Fig. 3.3   Life expectation in Great Britain, 1906 and 1985.
Source: CSO (1989), Table 7.2.

The changes in late-age mortality observed between 1961 and 1985 are reflected in increased life expectancy (see Table 3.8). Expressed in percentage terms the largest increases in life expectancy are illustrated by very elderly women. Between 1961 and 1985 men and women aged 65–74 years have recorded life expectancy increases of 11 per cent and 14 per cent respectively; for those aged 85 + the increases are 8 per cent for men and 20 per cent for women. In the US similar trends are evident with women aged 75 and over showing a 20.6 per cent increase in life expectancy between 1965 and 1985 (Verbrugge 1989).

There are variations in life expectancy within Great Britain. Smith and Jacobson (1988) report that expectation of life at birth for a male born in England and Wales in 1983/84 was 71.3 years compared with 69.9 years if he was born in Scotland. For women the expectations of life at birth were 77.4 and 75.9 years respectively.

In 1983 the expectation of life at birth in England and Wales was 71.3 years for men and 77.3 years for women (Whitehead 1987) compared with 55.3 and 54.4 years respectively for citizens of Bangladesh. Those born in countries referred to as the Third World are much less likely to reach what would be considered to be old age. However, the variations in mortality between the developed and Third World in the later years of life are much less extreme. Hoover and Siegel (1986) report that in Europe expectation of life at age 60 is 18.3 years compared with 14.1 in Africa and 14.3 in South Asia. Japan records the greatest life expectancy for both males and females.

Table 3.8   Expectation of life at different ages in Great Britain, 1906–85.

| | 1906 | | 1961 | | 1985 | | % change 1961–85 | |
	M	F	M	F	M	F	M	F
Birth	48.0	51.0	67.9	73.8	71.5	77.4	+5.3	+4.8
65	10.8	11.9	11.9	15.1	13.2	17.2	+10.9	+13.9
75	6.4	7.1	7.3	8.7	7.9	10.4	+8.2	+19.5

Source: CSO (1989), Table 7.2.

Social class and mortality

Inequality in health, especially that based on social class or occupational status, is a topic which has been subjected to considerable scrutiny. It is accepted that within any given population there are natural variations in health status. The inequalities in health debate has focused on identifying the extent to which socially generated variations in both health status and use of health services exist within and between populations. Although there is no consensus on the causes of inequality on health, their eradication is a policy common to the United Kingdom and the 33 other members of the European Region of the World Health Organization (WHO). In 1980 these countries committed themselves to the concept of health for all by the year 2000. The targets for this strategy were agreed in 1984, the first of which stated that

> by the year 2000, the actual difference in health status between countries and between groups within countries should be reduced by 25%, by improving the level of health of disadvantaged nations and groups.

The implications of what this should mean for older people have not been quantified.

THE BRITISH CONTEXT

The WHO programme of health for all by the year 2000 is a challenge to governments throughout the world to improve the health status of their populations. One important aspect of the health for all (HFA) approach is the reduction of inequalities arising from the concepts of age, class, ethnicity or gender or any combination of these dimensions.

Within Britain there are a variety of different ways of recording and classifying social class. The most frequently used is the Registrar General's classification which is based upon occupation. This divides the population into six main groups: class I (professional occupations such as the law); class II (senior managerial occupations); class IIIn non-manual (skilled non-manual occupations); class IIIm (skilled manual occupations); class IV (semi-skilled manual occupations); and class V (unskilled manual occupations). When examining class differences in mortality and morbidity it is usual to group together social classes I and II to form one category at the top of the class hierarchy and social classes IV and V to form the group at the lower end of the class distribution.

Inequalities in health status centring around the concept of social class are an enduring and pervasive feature of British society. Both the Black Report (DHSS 1980) and the *Health Divide* (Whitehead 1987) have indicated that the health experience of the population varies significantly with social class. The standardized mortality ratio (SMR) for males aged 20–64 for all causes in 1979 was 99 for non-manual workers and 129 for manual workers. For the period 1979–83 Townsend *et al.* (1988) report that for 65 out of 78 causes of death for men aged 20–64 in Britain the standardized mortality rate (SMR) is higher in classes IV and V than for classes I and II. The reverse gradient applies for only one cause of death, malignant melanoma of the skin. For women, out of 82 causes of death 62 demonstrate a classic social class gradient. Only a few causes of death for women illustrate a reverse class gradient (malignant neoplasm of the breast, malignant neoplasm of the brain, malignant melanoma of the skin and acute lymphoid leukaemia).

Within Britain the debate about the existence of class-based inequalities in health has become politically controversial. However, in academic terms, the debate has centred upon whether inequalities in health are increasing or decreasing. From a gerontological perspective this is a debate which has focused upon identifying inequalities in male deaths before the age of 65 years (i.e. premature male mortality). Rarely have researchers extended their analysis to consider inequalities within older age groups, possibly because they have implicitly or explicitly adopted a biological/medical framework which considers that old age is characterized by universal and inevitable ill health. Thus, inequalities in health status characteristic of the earlier phases of the life cycle are assumed to be overwhelmed by the biological process of ageing.

A significant disincentive to the consideration of social class and ageing are the problems surrounding the definition and quantification of social class for older people. A parallel may be drawn here with the debates surrounding the classification of class for women. Estes *et al.* (1984) observe that, at least in the United States, older people are seen as a separate social class defined in terms of a qualifying age and their formal withdrawal from the labour market. Such a perspective does not recognize the existence of internal variation within this group. However, it is clear that there are problems in developing a class taxonomy for older people. In Britain class is typically defined on the basis of occupation. This is problematic for a group which has no longer a part to play in the productive sector. Guillemard (1982) argues that we should widen our conceptualization of class to include typical lifetime trajectories which examine relationships to the means of consumption and production, and to the agencies of state. While conceptually this is an interesting development such measures would be difficult to operationalize. Thus in Britain we usually have to resort to a occupation-based definition.

Table 3.9 Standardized mortality ratios of males in Great Britain.

	15–64	*65–74*	*75+*
Class I	66	68	73
Class II	77	81	84
Class IIIn	105	86	92
Class IIIm	96	100	105
Class IV	109	106	108
Class V	124	109	116
Ratio – Class V/Class I	1.88	1.60	1.59

Source: Fox *et al.* (1985), Table 2.

In the United States research has shown that membership of a low social class group predicts a shorter life expectancy and higher death rates from all diseases. These findings are consistent across studies despite variations in methodology, ways of defining social class and populations studied. In the United States class is usually recorded in terms of income, level of education or occupation (or indeed some combination of these). For example, Estes *et al.* (1984) report that for those aged 65 + in 1974 reported activity limitation varied from 61.2 per cent of those with five years' or less education to 34.2 per cent of those with a college education.

MORTALITY AND SOCIAL CLASS

Evidence for class-based variations in mortality is provided by Fox *et al.* (1985). Using data from the OPCS longitudinal study they showed that, for males, class-based inequalities extended into later life. The SMR for males aged 65–74 from the professional and managerial classes (social classes I) was 68 compared with 109 for those from unskilled occupation groups (Table 3.9). The difference in the relative mortality of the extremes of the class hierarchy decrease with age. However, for those aged 75 + mortality among those in social class V is 59 per cent higher than for their counterparts in class I. These data would seem to indicate that, for men at least, social class differences in mortality remain a feature of later life.

Conclusion

Mortality data are the most readily available source of information about the health of the population. However, the information is limited in that it tells us only about those who have died. We must make inferences about the health status of the survivors from these data. Despite the limitations of mortality data it is possible to draw a number of conclusions about the distribution of health and illness in later life. First, there have been substantial improvements in mortality over this century which are reflected in increased life expectancy. These improvements in mortality are now almost totally confined to the first year of life and the years after age 65. Second, women have a longer expectation of life than men. Third, the main sources of mortality are cancers, circulatory diseases and respiratory diseases. The pattern of mortality is broadly similar for men and women. Fourth, there have been decreases in mortality for several major diseases, especially heart disease, stroke and respiratory disease. In contrast cancer mortality overall has changed little. More worryingly, mortality from lung cancer is still increasing. In the next chapter we consider morbidity patterns in later life and consider how far they reflect the patterns described by mortality data.

4 PHYSICAL HEALTH: PATTERNS OF MORBIDITY

Morbidity is a broad term used to describe non-mortal patterns of ill health within the population. Once again this is a limited way of examining health in that we are assuming that the distribution of health is the inverse of the pattern displayed by morbidity. In considering patterns of morbidity both within and between populations it is usual to distinguish between acute and chronic health problems.

The prevalence of acute health problems

Acute health problems are self-limiting conditions of short-term duration such as colds or flu or others with a defined span such as a broken leg. Such conditions may be much more amenable to medical intervention than chronic conditions. One source of data about self-reported acute health problems is the General Household Survey. The annual General Household Survey (GHS), is based upon a sample of approximately 10,000 households resident in Great Britain, and provides some data about the prevalence of acute and chronic health problems as well as considering the utilization of health and social care services. The GHS has been running since 1972 and is a large-scale survey designed to meet the information needs of a variety of different government departments.

The GHS includes a core of questions which appear in each year's survey. This is complemented by different years focusing upon specific topics or issues. For the gerontological research community the 1980 and 1985 GHS are of special interest as these years' surveys had a special section concerned with those aged 65 +. These sections looked in detail at activities of daily living and the provision of additional help. The 1985 GHS also included a special set of questions concerning informal care. Secondary analysis of these data and published tables are used extensively in this book.

Each year the GHS asks 'in the 14 days prior to interview have you had to cut down on any of the things you usually do (about the house/at work or in your

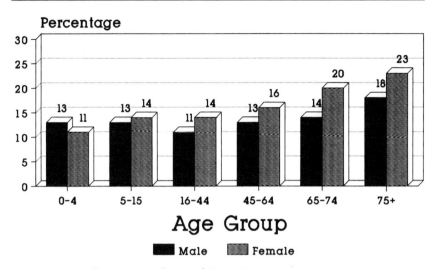

Fig. 4.1   Acute illness in population of Great Britain, 1987.
Source: OPCS (1988b), Table 4.1.

free time) because of illness or injury?' Those who report restricted activity are
then asked for how many days they have had to reduce their activities. From
GHS data we may therefore calculate the prevalence of self-reported acute
health episodes and the duration of these episodes.

In 1987 14 per cent of the population of Great Britain, 16 per cent of females
and 12 per cent of males, reported that they had had an acute health episode in
the previous 14 days. As might be expected from the study of mortality data
acute health problems are not equally distributed throughout the population.
The self-reported prevalence of acute illness, as defined by restricted activity
due to a health problem in the 14 days before interview, increases with age from
12 per cent for the population aged 15–44 to 21 per cent of those aged 75 +
(Figure 4.1). Although the prevalence of acute health problems does seem to
increase somewhat with age only a minority of those aged 75 + report the
presence of such a health problem.

Another way of examining acute illness prevalence is to consider specific
acute health problems and the extent to which their prevalence increases (or
decreases) with age. Detailed symptom data are available from the health and
lifestyle survey (HLS); a large scale survey of the adult population of Great
Britain undertaken in 1984–85 (Table 4.1). These data show an age-related
increase in the reported prevalence of only some of these symptoms. For
example, the percentage reporting that they had had a cold or flu in the
previous month showed little change with age. However, among the older age
groups there was a very marked gender difference in the prevalence of these
symptoms; 43 per cent of women aged 65–74 report that they suffered from
painful joints compared with 28 per cent of males.

Table 4.1 Prevalence of selected conditions in the last month of population aged 65 + in Great Britain (%), 1985.

| | 65–74 | | 75 + | |
	M	F	M	F
Painful joints	28	43	34	43
Breathlessness	22	28	26	31
Bad back	17	28	25	31
Trouble with feet	16	23	23	36
Trouble with eyes	15	27	24	38
Trouble with ears	21	17	22	21
Faints/dizziness	8	11	10	18
Constipation	14	13	13	22
Cough	14	12	13	10
Sinus/catarrh	16	17	16	16
Indigestion	21	23	18	23
Headache	13	25	13	23
Colds/flu	26	27	27	26
N	448	512	231	344

Source: Cox *et al.* (1987), Table 2.6.

Chronic health problems

Chronic health problems and disability are long term and are not usually curable, although medical intervention may alleviate some, or all, of the associated symptoms. A typical example of such a long-term health problem is arthritis. It is these types of health problems which are perceived as being an integral, inevitable and universal feature of old age. Estimating the prevalence of such conditions within the population is, however, problematic as this depends both upon the methods of study used and the threshold used to define disability.

WHAT IS DISABILITY?

A major problem in research when considering chronic health problems is that of terminology; words such as disability are frequently used in popular discourse, legislation and academic research with a resultant confusion over precise meaning. One useful tool for thinking more clearly about the whole concept of chronic ill health is the international classification of impairments, disabilities and handicaps. This distinguishes three key concepts: impairment, disability and handicap.

Impairment describes parts or systems of the body which do not function properly such as hearing or sight. Disability refers to restrictions or lack of ability to undertake activities considered normal. Thus disability relates to things people cannot do such as going to work, cooking or participating in sporting activities. Handicap refers to the disadvantage experienced by an individual as a result of the impairment or disability. For example, poor eyesight (an impairment) may result in poor vision (a disability) which might result in the person failing to gain employment (handicap).

The position is a little more complex than this simple schema suggests. Not all impairments result in disability. Although a large proportion of the population has visual impairment the availability of appropriate glasses or contact lenses means that a much lower percentage of the population has a visual disability. It is also important to remember that a single impairment may give rise to numerous disabilities. The relationship between disability and handicap is rather more complex as this is related to the physical environment, the availability of helpers and the kinds of social role that the individual is expected to fulfil.

THE PREVALENCE OF CHRONIC HEALTH PROBLEMS: GHS DATA

The annual General Household Survey has always included a question about chronic health problems in its researches. The GHS uses a two-stage approach to identify those with chronic health problems. First, respondents are asked if they have any long standing illness, disability or infirmity. This is subsequently referred to as long standing illness. Second, those who report the presence of such a condition are then asked if it limits their activities in any way. This is referred to as long standing limiting illness. In 1987 33 per cent of the population, 35 per cent of females and 32 per cent of males, reported the presence of a long standing illness. The prevalence of this type of health problem increases steadily with age so that 72 per cent of those aged 75 + report this type of health problem (see Figure 4.2).

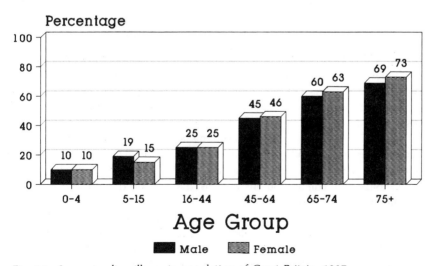

Fig. 4.2   Long standing illness in population of Great Britain, 1987.
Source: OPCS (1988b), Table 4.1.

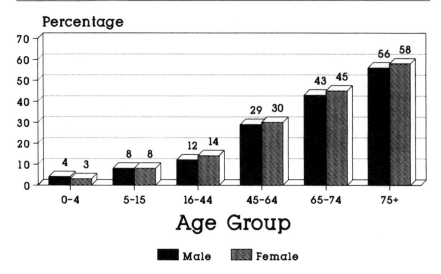

Fig. 4.3 Long standing limiting illness in population of Great Britain, 1987.
Source: OPCS (1988b), Table 4.1.

Not all of those with a long standing illness report that it restricts their activity. Consequently 21 per cent of the population of Great Britain report that they have a long standing limiting illness (19 per cent of males and 22 per cent of females). The proportion of the population reporting a limiting illness increases with age (Figure 4.3). However, it is worth noting that, even among the very oldest age group, almost half of the population do not report the presence of this type of health problem.

THE PREVALENCE OF DISABILITY: THE OPCS DISABILITY SURVEY

Studies of the prevalence of disability in the community are influenced by both study design and the way that the questions are asked. To illustrate this point the disability prevalence estimates for those living in private households generated by the GHS question on long standing limiting illness and the OPCS disability survey were compared (see Figure 4.4).

The OPCS disability survey was commissioned in 1984 and consists of four separate surveys carried out betwen 1985 and 1988. These surveys covered adults in private households, adults in institutions, children in private households and children in institutions. Details of the methodology are described by Martin *et al.* (1988).

The overall disability prevalence rates generated by the OPCS disability survey are lower than those produced by the GHS: 208 per 1000 population aged 16 + compared with 135 per 1000. For those aged 75 + the pattern is reversed: i.e. the GHS data produce lower disability prevalence estimates

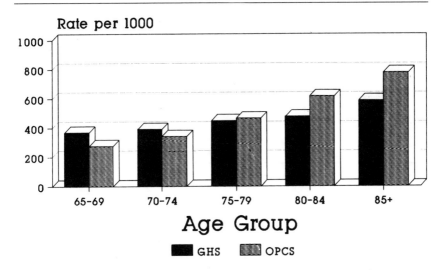

Fig. 4.4   Disability and chronic illness prevalence by age in population aged 65 +, 1988.
Source: Martin *et al.* (1988), Table 3.5.

(Figure 4.4). For example, the OPCS disability estimated prevalence for those aged 85 + is 32 per cent higher than that produced by the GHS: 779 per 1000 population compared with 588 per 1000. This difference probably reflects the variation in questions and methodology used in the two surveys. One instance of this is that the GHS question asks about restrictions of activity. Many older people may consider any limitations of activity which they experience to be a result of old age rather than a chronic health problem.

These differences between the estimates of the prevalence of disability in two large-scale and well conducted surveys serve to remind us that there is no absolute and 'correct' disability prevalence estimate. This reflects the point made earlier that disability is a continuum and that the threshold at which disability is defined determines the prevalence rate.

HOW MANY DISABLED PEOPLE ARE THERE?

The OPCS disability survey estimated that there were six million people in Great Britain with one or more disabilities (see Table 4.2). The vast majority of this population, almost 70 per cent, were aged 60 or over. This means that approximately 4,275,000 adults aged 60 and over have some form of disability, using the OPCS definition. The absolute number of adults classed as disabled increases continuously with age up to 79 years and then decreases slightly. This decrease reflects the lower numbers of people in the population aged 80 +. When expressed as a rate there is a continuous increase in disability with age.

Table 4.2   Estimates of disabled adults in Great Britain, 1988.

| | Numbers (000) | | | Rate per 1000 | |
	Private households	*Communal establishments*	*Total*	*Private households*	*Total*
60–69	1298	36	1334	236	240
70–79	1589	98	1687	395	408
80 +	1037	217	1254	674	714
All ages	5780	422	6202	135	142

Source: Martin *et al.* (1988), Tables 3.3. and 3.4.

WHERE DO THE DISABLED ELDERLY LIVE?

Of the 6,202,000 adults defined as disabled, 422,000 (7 per cent) lived in some form of institutional care. At all ages the vast majority of those defined as disabled reside in the community; institutional care caters only for a minority of this population. The percentage of those with disabilities living outside the community is greatest for those aged 80 + where 17 per cent live in institutions (see Table 4.2).

DISABILITY PREVALENCE: COMMUNITY AND INSTITUTIONS

The GHS is a survey which considers only those resident in the community; residents of institutions are excluded. Thus prevalence estimates based upon the GHS will under-report the true prevalence by excluding a highly dependent and disabled group. However, it is difficult to generate accurate disability prevalence for the institutional population as the total number of those resident remains unknown. Without some idea of the denominator it is impossible to calculate a prevalence rate. Consequently it is not possible to calculate separate community and institution disability prevalence rates.

The OPCS disability survey included both institutions and a community sample from which overall disability prevalence estimates are generated. Inclusion of the institutional population will increase the estimated prevalence at each group. For example, the prevalence of disability for those aged 80 + is 674 per 1000 population when only private households are considered and 714 per 1000 when the institutional population is included (see Table 4.2). Inclusion of the institutional population appears to increase the overall disability prevalence rate by about 6 per cent.

THE SEVERITY OF DISABILITY

As well as estimating the number of people with disability it is important to have some indication of the severity of those disabilities. The OPCS survey asked about the ability to undertake a variety of specific activities; it did not ask about severity of limitation. Indeed this would have been difficult to achieve within its methodology. The survey has therefore developed its own severity scale to summarize the extent of disability. This was a complex undertaking as the scale had to compare limitations within broadly similar disability areas, compare severity between different types of disability and assess the severity of different combinations of disability. Martin *et al.* (1988) describe the procedure used to develop the severity scale which ranges from 1 (least disabled) to 10 (most disabled).

While there are obviously problems in developing and using this type of notional scale it has some utility. Several points may be considered from an examination of the distribution of disability severity. First, overall there are more people in the least disabled category than in the more severe category (see Table 4.3). For example, there were 1,186,000 adults in private households classified in severity category 1 compared with 102,000 in category 10. Changing the definition of disability so that the severity class 1 was excluded would reduce the number of disabled people in the population from 6,202,000 to 5,004,000 (a reduction of 1,198,000)! Second, the pattern of disability differs between institutions and private households. In the community the pattern reflects that described above: there are more people in the least disabled categories. In institutions the pattern is reversed so that there are 13,000 adults in institutions in severity group 1 and 108,000 in category 10. It is only for the most severe disability class that the majority, 51 per cent , live in some form of institutional care. Third, older people are over-represented in the more severe disability groups: those aged 60+ constitute 75 per cent of the most severe disability group but only 64 per cent of the least severe category.

Table 4.3 Estimates of disabled adults by severity in Great Britain (000), 1988.

Severity category	Private households				Communal establishments			
	60–69	70–79	80+	Total all ages	65–69	70–79	80+	Total all ages
10	15	23	39	102	7	24	58	108
9	57	68	93	285	7	18	45	80
8	59	92	87	338	5	12	30	58
7	78	115	123	447	3	9	22	39
6	85	149	107	511	2	9	18	34
5	146	176	132	679	2	6	15	29
4	152	179	105	676	3	8	12	27
3	173	212	109	732	2	6	8	19
2	225	263	105	824	2	5	6	16
1	308	310	138	1186	3	3	3	13
Total	1298	1589	1037	5780	36	98	217	422

Source: Martin *et al.* (1988), Table 3.3.

Table 4.4   The prevalence of different types of disability in Great Britain, 1988.

| Disability type | Rate per 1000 | | | | Estimated numbers | | | |
| | Private households | | Total | | Private households | | Communal establishments | |
	60–74	75+	60–74	75+	60–74	75+	60–74	75+
Locomotion	195	464	198	496	1520	1511	45	247
Reaching and stretching	52	129	54	149	404	422	22	107
Dexterity	76	180	78	199	589	585	24	120
Seeing	52	225	56	262	405	732	40	198
Hearing	108	307	110	328	843	1000	28	161
Personal care	93	263	99	313	728	856	53	253
Continence	38	120	42	147	299	393	31	128
Communication	38	112	42	140	296	365	36	129
Behaviour	36	88	40	152	280	287	31	98
Intellectual function	37	107	40	109	286	349	47	188
Consciousness	4	6	10	9	33	19	8	12
Eating and drinking	11	18	12	30	83	59	12	45
Disfigurement	18	27	—	—	141	87	—	—

Source: Martin *et al.* (1988), Tables 3.13 and 3.14.

THE PREVALENCE OF DIFFERENT TYPES OF DISABILITY

Disability is not a unitary concept. Rather there are a variety of different dimensions of disability. The OPCS disability survey (Martin *et al.* 1988) considered 13 different aspects of disability ranging from difficulties with locomotion to problems with consciousness, eating and drinking and disfigurement (Table 4.4). In both absolute and relative terms locomotion, i.e. mobility difficulties, were the most common. Overall the OPCS survey indicates that 3,323,000 people aged 60 and over have problems with mobility. However, this does not give any indication as to how much the individual is handicapped by this problem. Although not all elderly obviously experience mobility problems this is clearly an extensive problem for older people. Within each type of disability there is a consistent pattern of the prevalence rate increasing with age. Again within each type of disability the majority of those who experience the problem reside in the community.

IS THE PREVALENCE OF DISABILITY INCREASING?

The data provided suggest that in all cases the prevalence of morbidity increases significantly with age. However, it is important to emphasize that,

Table 4.5   Trends in self-reported health in Great Britain (%), 1974–87.

	Long standing limiting illness						Acute illness					
	65–74		75 +		All ages		65–74		75 +		All ages	
Year	M	F	M	F	M	F	M	F	M	F	M	F
1974	33	38	39	49	13	15	10	13	11	14	9	10
1976	38	40	48	53	15	17	9	11	10	11	9	10
1979	37	38	45	54	16	18	12	16	17	22	12	14
1980	39	42	45	54	16	19	11	17	15	21	11	13
1981	35	41	44	56	18	20	12	19	17	20	11	14
1982	41	39	43	54	16	18	13	18	17	23	11	14
1983	40	45	53	54	18	21	15	18	17	21	22	14
1987	43	45	56	58	19	22	14	20	18	20	12	16

Source: OPCS (1988b), Table 9.1.

even in the very oldest age groups, ill health is not a universal feature of later life. Several factors may account for this observation. Selection effects may ensure that only the fittest survive to experience old age. Second, our expectation that all elderly are ill is clearly misplaced. However, this conclusion must be interpreted with caution. The suggested increase in prevalence of morbidity with age is based in this case upon cross-sectional data. Methodologically this is flawed as cohort influences such as patterns of smoking and other behavioural factors, diet, privation in childhood and access to, and quality of, medical care may also be important. Using a longitudinal methodology, Milne (1985) and Jagger et al. (1989) among others have demonstrated an age-related increase in morbidity. However, when making projections about the health status of future generations of elderly it is important to recognize that cohort effects may be very influential. Today's elderly experienced great hardship and deprivation during their formative years. Furthermore, they did not have the same access to health services that future generations will have received.

The analysis of trends over time offers another indirect method of considering age and cohort related effects upon health. The prevalence of long-standing limiting illness, as recorded by the GHS, is increasing across all age and sex groups (Table 4.5). A similar trend is evident for acute health problems. This would mean that each successive cohort entering old age would be less healthy than its predecessors. However, it is not possible to make this inference from the data as they are based upon subjects' responses to a single question. The apparent changes in the prevalence of health problems may reflect changes in peoples' expectations about their health as well as real changes in the prevalence of chronic health problems. Changes in the question wording used also make the meaningful interpretation of time series health data problematic.

Table 4.6 Estimated numbers of disabled elderly in Great Britain, 1990–2025.

| Age group | Total numbers (000) | | Numbers disabled (000) | | | |
| | | | 1990 | | 2025 | |
	1988	2025	GHS*	OPCS**	GHS	OPCS
65–69	2854	3023	1053	784	1115	831
70–74	2168	2640	847	741	1032	902
75–79	1843	2255	827	858	1012	1050
80–84	1170	1294	552	720	617	797
85+	769	1256	452	599	738	978

*1985 age specific using prevalence of long standing limiting illness.
**Using disability prevalence from OPCS disability survey.

HOW MANY DISABLED ELDERLY WILL THERE BE IN THE FUTURE?

Predicting the numbers of disabled elderly into the future is problematic as it depends upon the projection forward of current patterns of disability. It is possible that future cohorts of older people will illustrate different patterns of disability. There is an additional problem which centres upon the choice of the disability prevalence used for projection. As was illustrated earlier, two well conducted surveys of chronic health problems produced differing prevalence rates; the inclusion (or exclusion) of the institutionalized population within the prevalence rate will also influence the resultant prediction.

In 1988 there were, according to the GHS long-standing limiting illness prevalence estimate, 3,373,100 people aged 65 + classed as disabled compared with 3,702,000 using the OPCS survey estimate (see Table 4.6). Projecting these rates forward to 2025 reveals that there would be 4,514,000 people aged 65 + with chronic health problems using the GHS data and 4,558,000 using the OPCS estimate. Both estimates suggest a significant increase in the numbers of elderly with chronic health problems in the early decades of next century. However, these are only projections of current trends and we cannot be certain that current levels of morbidity will be reproduced by future generations of elderly.

WHAT ARE THE CAUSES OF DISABILITY?

We have indicated that disability is fairly prevalent amongst the older age groups. What are the causes of these disabling conditions? Mortality data indicated that cancer, circulatory diseases and respiratory diseases were the biggest causes of death. Are these the main causes of disability? The OPCS disability survey provides some indication of the main causes of disability and suggests that these vary between adults in private households and those in institutions. For those in private households 46 per cent of disabled adults

Table 4.7 Causes of disability in adults in Great Britain (%)*, 1988.

ICD chapter	Private householder	Communal establishment
Infections	1	0
Neoplasms	2	4
Endocrine	2	8
Blood disorders	1	2
Mental	13	56
Nervous system	13	30
Eye	22	17
Ear	38	13
Circulatory	20	16
Respiratory	13	6
Digestive	6	10
Genito-urinary	3	10
Skin	1	2
Musculo-skeletal	46	37
Congenital	0	0
Other	6	10

*Percentages do not total 100 as some respondents had more than one complaint.
Source: Martin *et al.* (1988).

reported disorders of the musculo-skeletal system, while 56 per cent of those in institutions reported mental disorders (see Table 4.7). A similar pattern has been reported for North America. The pattern of disabling conditions does not show any significant differences between the sexes.

The main causes of mortality among the older age groups were not the most important causes of morbidity. Consequently inferences made about the main sources of morbidity in later life drawn from mortality data will be misleading. Important sources of mortality such as cancer are not significant sources of disability. Conversely, musculo-skeletal problems, which account for few deaths of those aged 65 +, are a major cause of disability in the community.

THE PREVALENCE OF HANDICAP

As noted earlier handicap describes the disadvantage resulting from disability or impairment. Data from the health and lifestyle survey indicate that for those aged 65–74 43 per cent of men and 39 per cent of women with a chronic health problem report that it does not restrict their activities, or handicap them. At the opposite extreme 14 per cent of men aged 75 + and 30 per cent of women are rendered house bound because of their disability (see Figure 4.5). Of those who reported that their disability handicapped them in some way, 90 per cent stated that they 'had to take special care' and 86 per cent reported a restricted work or social life. This confirms the well observed inverse relationship between disability and social contact.

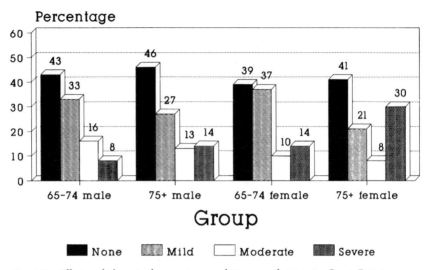

Fig. 4.5   Effects of chronic disease in population aged 65 + in Great Britain, 1984–5.
Source: Health and Lifestyle Survey (1987) – an analysis of unpublished data.

Disability prevalence: activities of daily living

The investigation of disability in later life may be developed further by considering the ability to undertake a variety of activities and tasks considered essential to an independent life in the community. Researchers typically focus upon personal care tasks (e.g. washing, dressing and feeding) and houshold management activities, or instrumental activities, such as shopping or cleaning. It is also usual to include information about aspects of mobility such as getting around the house and coping with steps and stairs. Studies which have examined the ability of older people to undertake activities of daily living (adl) usually take one of two main approaches. The first attempts to identify how much difficulty a person has performing a specific task while the second approach considers whether help is received in order to undertake specific tasks. The focus of this latter approach is of enumerating the dependency of the older age groups.

For the population aged 65 + the vast majority are able to cope with outdoor mobility and getting around the house (see Table 4.8). In terms of personal care less than 10 per cent have problems bathing, washing or feeding; however, almost one-third, 29 per cent, have problems cutting their toenails. Of the instrumental daily living activities jobs involving cleaning pose problems for about 20 per cent, while cooking is a problem for less than 10 per cent. There

Table 4.8 Inability to undertake mobility, self-care and domestic tasks in Great Britain (%), 1985.

			Age			
	65–69	70–74	75–79	80–84	85+	All 65+
Walk out of doors	5	7	14	24	47	13
Getting up and down stairs and steps	4	5	10	17	31	9
Getting around the house (on the level)	1	1	2	3	6	2
Getting to the toilet	1	1	2	2	7	2
Getting in and out of bed	1	1	3	2	7	2
Cut toenails	16	24	34	48	65	29
Bathing, showering, washing all over	4	5	10	16	31	9
Brushing hair (females), shaving (males)	1	1	1	3	7	2
Washing face and hands	0	1	1	1	3	1
Feeding	0	1	0	1	2	1
Household shopping	7	10	16	29	56	16
Wash paintwork	8	13	24	34	62	20
Clean windows inside	9	13	21	34	63	19
Clean and sweep floors	5	7	13	20	45	12
Job involving climbing	17	25	36	52	76	31
Wash clothing by hand	4	5	9	12	32	8
Open screw-top jars	7	7	11	15	29	10
Cook a main meal	4	4	9	13	29	8
Use a frying pan	2	2	5	8	19	5
Make a cup of tea	1	1	3	3	8	2
N	1062	1025	788	395	240	3510

Source: OPCS (1988a), Tables 12.14, 12.31, 12.33 and 12.37.

is obviously a hierarchy of tasks implicit within this list; difficulties with cleaning will be fairly common but problems with feeding much rarer.

The percentage of those aged 65 + reporting problems with these adl tasks does increase substantially with age irrespective of the task under review. For example, 17 per cent of those aged 65–69 and 76 per cent of those aged 85 + have problems with tasks which involve climbing.

HAS THE PREVALENCE OF ADL PROBLEMS CHANGED OVER TIME?

There are few longitudinal studies which have published data describing changes in the ability to undertake specific adl activities over time. Comparison of three national surveys carried out between 1976 and 1985 reveals very little change in the percentage of older people reporting difficulties with a plethora of adl activities (see Table 4.9).

Table 4.9   Inability to undertake personal, mobility, self-care and domestic tasks in population aged 65(%).

	1976	GHS 1980	GHS 1985
Walk out of doors	13	12	13
Getting up and down stairs and steps	6	8	0
Getting around the house (on the level)	2	2	2
Getting to the toilet	2	2	2
Getting in and out of bed	2	2	2
Cut toenails	25	28	29
Bathing, showering, washing all over	16	9	9
Brushing hair (females), shaving (males)	2	2	2
Washing face and hands	1	2	1
Feeding	1	0	1
Wash paintwork	24	18	20
Clean windows inside	24	17	19
Clean and sweep floors	11	10	12
Job involving climbing	43	33	31
Wash clothing by hand	15	7	8
Open screw-top jars	10	10	10
Cook a main meal	9	7	8
Use a frying pan	5	4	5
Make a cup of tea	3	2	2

Source: Tinker (1984), Table 10.44.

HOW MANY ELDERLY IN THE FUTURE WILL HAVE ADL PROBLEMS?

Grossing up the responses to the 1985 GHS adl questions reveals that approximately 2,500,000 people aged 65 + have problems in cutting their toenails (see Table 4.10). Household maintenance activities such as cleaning windows or domestic chores such as shopping represent a problem for approximately 1,500,000, while a much smaller number, about 170,000 have severe mobility problems in, e.g., getting to the toilet. Again, projection forward of these rates to the year 2025 suggests that there will be a significant increase in the numbers of older people requiring help with personal and house care activities.

Gender variations in morbidity

Women over 65 experience both worse acute and chronic health than their male counterparts (Table 4.11). This could simply be an artefact of the differential age

Table 4.10 Need for care: estimated number of people aged 65 + unable to undertake selected adl activities in Great Britain (000), 1981–2025.

Activity	1981	2025
Getting up/down stairs	765	1017
Getting to the toilet	170	226
Cutting toenails	2465	3277
Bathing/showering	765	1017
Household shopping	1360	1808
Cleaning windows	1615	2147

Based upon population data in Table 2.1 and prevalence data in Table 4.8.

Table 4.11 Morbidity by sex of population aged 65 + in Great Britain, 1985.

	Crude %		Standardized*	
	Male	Female	Male	Female
Long standing limiting illness	41	45	90	108
Acute illness	15	21	81	119
N	1436	2090	—	—

*Standardized for age using indirect method.
Source: General Household Survey (1985) – own analysis of unpublished data.

distribution of the sexes for, as we saw in Chapter 2, there are more women in the very elderly age groups. Standardization is a statistical technique which takes into account the differential age distribution (see Table 4.11) and this suggests that older women do indeed experience more ill health than males of the same age. Such findings have also been reported in North America (Verbrugge 1989).

It is well documented that men are less likely to survive to old age than women. The morbidity data presented demonstrated higher prevalence of chronic health problems among women as compared with men. It therefore seems that sex differences in health status are characteristic of the whole of the lifecourse. Although women are more likely to survive to old age than men they are more likely than men to experience chronic ill health.

Again there are several explanations posited to account for these gender differences in health status. Three explanations suggest that the observed difference is an artefact of social structure because

• women are more willing to report symptoms;
• it is 'easier' for women to go sick because they have fewer social roles; or
• fewer constraints.

The fourth explanation accepts that the gender difference in morbidity is real and results because women have more commitments and work harder than

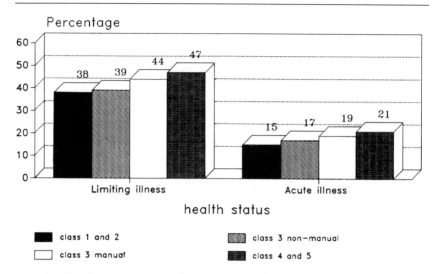

Fig. 4.6   Health by social class of population aged 65 + in Great Britain 1985.
Source: General Household Survey (1985) – an analysis of unpublished data.

men. It seems likely that several factors account for the gender differences in morbidity and that there are different explanations for different types of illness.

Morbidity and social class

There are significant differences between social classes in the prevalence of chronic and acute ill health (Figure 4.6). Those elderly from social classes 1 and 2 illustrate a prevalence of long standing limiting illness which is 20 per cent lower than that recorded by their counterparts from classes 4 and 5. Standardization to take into account the differing age and gender composition of the class groups indicates that the observed variations are not simply an artefact of the differential age and sex composition of the social class groups (Table 4.12). Consistently, those elderly from the professional and managerial classes experience better health than their contemporaries from the manual occupation groups.

Policy implications

Current evidence indicates that older people are more healthy than popular stereotypes suggest. It appears that for acute health problems older people are little different, in terms of prevalence, from younger age groups. However, it is clear that chronic health problems appear to increase with age. Most of the

Table 4.12   Morbidity by social class of population aged 65 + in Great Britain, 1985.

| | Standardized health ratio* | |
	Classes I & II	Classes IV & V
Long standing limiting illness	90	111
Acute illness	85	115
N	824	985

*Standardized for age and sex.
Source: GHS (1985) – own analysis of unpublished data.

evidence is based upon cross-sectional data and must, therefore, be interpreted cautiously. The current scenario of an ageing population suggests that we can expect an increase in disability prevalence as the elderly population itself ages.

However, there is much uncertainty about the health of future cohorts of elderly. Will they be as disabled as current cohorts? Will the extreme gender differences in health status continue? Will current class inequalities in health continue to be important? Improved data are required before these questions can be answered with any certainty.

Indeed, comparison of the 1980 and 1985 GHS data suggests that there may indeed be differences between cohorts in the prevalence of chronic health problems. If confirmed by longitudinal analysis this would indicate that the ageing of the population over the next decade need not automatically bring an increase in the number of people with health problems and who require care. This observation would also support Fries's compression of morbidity thesis (1980).

5 MENTAL HEALTH IN LATER LIFE

Having considered the methodological issues and epidemiological terms for describing disease in population this chapter is concerned with the mental health of older people. Dementia is the mental disorder most usually associated with the later parts of the life cycle. The epidemiology of this condition is considered in detail in this chapter. However, this chapter also includes other aspects of mental health including the affective disorders such as anxiety and depression and less clinically defined dimensions of mental health.

Dementia

Much of the literature concerned with ageing focuses upon notions such as satisfaction, adjustment and other terms describing individual psychological and social well being (Coleman 1988). The frequency of use of these terms suggests that ageing and, more specifically, old age is the most problematic phase of the life course. This rather negative view of later life is especially common when we consider mental health and, specifically, dementia. The labels most readily ascribed to an older person are 'demented' or 'senile'. Slater and Gearing (1988) suggest that these negative views of mental health in later life are held by professionals as well as the wider society. Slater and Gearing (1988) give the following quotation from Samuel Johnson, written in the eighteeenth century, to illustrate their argument that we are too ready to ascribe the label demented to older people. Dr Johnson wrote

> There is a wicked inclination in most people to suppose an old man decayed in his intellects. If a young or middle aged man, when leaving company, does not recollect where he has laid his hat, it is nothing; but if the same inattention is discovered in an old man, people will shrug their shoulders and say, 'his memory is going'.

Dementia may be defined as the global impairment of higher mental functioning including the loss of memory, problem solving ability, the use of

Table 5.1   The importance of different types of dementia in two British studies (%).

	Hospital*	*Community***
Alzheimers disease	39	32
Multi-infarct	44	49
Other	17	19

Source: *Gaspar (1980); **Kay *et al.* (1964).

learned skills, the loss of social skills and emotional control. The consciousness of the sufferer is not impaired. In the most general of terms this condition is both progressive and irreversible.

Dementia is a complex state and not every person who experiences the disease will present the complete spectrum of symptoms. Despite the use of dementia as a global term, it is not a single condition. Rather there are a variety of different disease states which may produce the dementia syndrome. These include Alzheimers disease, which was first described in 1907, multiple brain infarctions (small strokes in the brain), drug toxity and Huntington's Chorea.

HOW FREQUENT ARE THESE DIFFERENT TYPES OF DEMENTING CONDITIONS?

This is a very difficult question to answer authoritatively as accurate diagnosis of the different types of dementia is often difficult and may not, in many cases, be confirmed without a post mortem. In both hospital and community populations Alzheimers disease and multi-infarc dementia are the two major causes of dementing conditions (Table 5.1). Specific causes such as tumours, drug toxicity, infection and trauma appear to be of lesser significance as causes of dementia. However, at a clinical level such factors need to be excluded when examining a patient suspected of having dementia.

These data must, however, only be taken as very approximate guides as to the probable distribution of causes of dementia as studies have not standardized the way they define and collect their information. Given the difficulty of identifying the different types of dementia it is usual for epidemiological studies of this disease to concentrate upon organic brain failure as a single condition. Rarely can community surveys, for example, differentiate between the different disease types. This concentration upon identifying broad trends in the epidemiology of organic brain disorders is reflected in the sections of this chapter dealing with incidence and prevalence.

The prevalence of dementia in later life

How common is dementia among the older age groups? As is indicated in the following sections it is not easy to answer this alarmingly simple question. The

rate per million

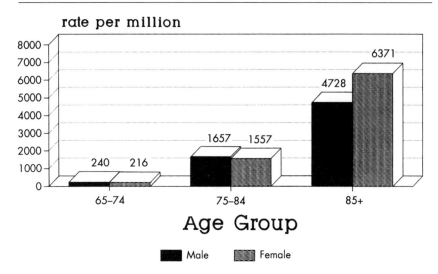

Fig. 5.1   Dementia mortality rates of population aged 65 + in England and Wales, 1987.
Source: OPCS (1989b), Table 3.

freedom with which the epithet 'senile' is attributed to the old, but especially old ladies, might give the impression that the disease is virtually universal among all those over 65. One possible way of attempting to establish the prevalence of dementia is via the analysis of death certificate data.

DEMENTIA MORTALITY

In 1987 in England and Wales there were 9,572 deaths attributable to senile and pre-senile dementia, of which 488 were of the pre-senile type (OPCS 1989b). The vast majority, 95 per cent, of deaths certified as due to dementia were among those aged 65 + . Dementia death rates increase with age and are very similar between the sexes, with the exception of those aged 85 + where rates are considerably higher for females as compared with males (Figure 5.1). While death certificates are a convenient source of epidemiological data, their validity for the study of the dementing diseases is questionable. Martyn and Pippard (1988) examined the death certificates of 117 people who were diagnosed as demented whilst alive. Dementia was recorded as the cause of death for 22 per cent of cases and mentioned on 57 per cent of certificates. This evidence indicates that mortality data are of little use when trying to establish the prevalence of the dementing illnesses as they are almost certainly a significant underestimate of the true prevalence of the condition.

COMMUNITY STUDIES OF DEMENTIA PREVALENCE: METHODS OF
MEASUREMENT

The dementing illnesses are the most researched aspect of mental health in later
life. Henderson (1990) reports that there have been over 50 population studies
of dementia prevalence and Jorm *et al.* (1987) have comprehensively reviewed
47 such studies. In Britain there have been a number of different community
dementia studies conducted in a diverse number of locations including
Liverpool, Nottingham, Melton Mowbray and Newcastle, which have
attempted to establish the prevalence of dementia among older people.

In attempting to establish the prevalence of dementia a variety of different
instruments have been used to identify the presence/absence of the condition.
Recent British studies of dementia prevalence have largely relied upon the
twelve-item information/orientation scale from the Clifton Assessment Procedures for the Elderly (CAPE) (Pattie and Gilleard 1979). The scale was originally
developed to distinguish organic and functional mental disorders in a hospital
population of older people. Subsequently this scale has been used in Melton
Mowbray by Jagger *et al.* (1989) and Nottingham by Morgan *et al.* (1987). The
twelve items in the scale are shown in Table 5.2 and include questions about an
individual's awareness of both time and place. The brevity of the scale and its
general acceptability in community survey settings are the two main factors
underlying its popularity.

Responses to the individual items are scored. The scale has a range from 0 to
12. Correct answers are scored 1 and incorrect answers score 0. A score of 7/8
or below is usually used as the cut-off point to define the presence of dementia.
The validity of this scale has been considered by studies in both hospital (Pattie
and Gilleard 1975, 1976) and community settings (Morgan *et al.* 1987). These

Table 5.2   Instruments used to identify dementia prevalence.

*Items of the information/orientation scale of the Clifton Assessment Schedule (Pattie & Gilleard
(1975))*

  1 What is your name/full name?
  2 How old are you?
  3 What is your date of birth?
  4 What is this place/Where are you now?
  5 What is the name of this hospital/What is the address of this place?
  6 What is the name of this town/city?
  7 Who is the Prime Minister?
  8 Who is the President of the USA?
  9 What are the colours of the national flag/Union Jack?
 10 What day is it?
 11 What month is it?
 12 What year is it?

validity studies compared clinical opinion as to whether a respondent showed signs of dementia with their score upon the scale.

Copeland *et al.* (1976) devised the geriatric mental state (GMS). This was a broad ranging psychiatric questionnaire which covered a variety of aspects of mental health. The information collected by this standardized set of questions was then presented to a clinician for a diagnosis. A computer algorithm, AGECAT, has now been developed to undertake this task (Copeland *et al.* 1987). The data from the GMS are put into 157 symptom groups which are then gathered into eight clusters. This index distinguishes five different levels of organic brain syndrome ranging from severe to subclinical.

COMMUNITY STUDIES OF DEMENTIA PREVALENCE: RESULTS

Of the extensive number of community dementia studies undertaken in Britain 10 are reviewed in Table 5.3. These dementia prevalence studies have produced overall rates ranging from 2.5 per cent to 9.3 per cent of those studied. Estimates of the prevalence of severe dementia also show a variation from 1 per cent to 6 per cent of those studied.

WHY DO THESE PREVALENCE ESTIMATES VARY SO WIDELY?

As was discussed in Chapter 1 the notion of prevalence depends crucially upon the unambiguous classification of the study population into cases (i.e. those with dementia) and non-cases (i.e. those without dementia). The first important point in interpreting these wide differences in prevalence estimates between studies is the method used to define dementia. It seems likely that dementia is the extreme end of a continuum of behaviour; the point prevalence is to some degree determined by where the case definition line is drawn. The concept of

Table 5.3   Major recent British studies of dementia prevalence, 1975–87.

Author	Date	Age	Sample	Overall prevalence (%)	Severe dementia (%)
Bond *et al.*	1982	65+	808	8.1	—
Clarke *et al.*	1986	75+	1203	4.5	—
Copeland *et al.*	1987	65+	1070	5.2	—
Gilmore	1977	65+	300	9.3	1.0
Gruer	1975	65+	762	8.3	—
Gurland *et al.*	1983	65+	396	2.5	2.5
Kay *et al.*	1964	65+	758	8.8	6.2
Maule *et al.*	1984	62+	487	8.6	0.6
Morgan *et al.*	1987	65+	1042	3.2	—
Vetter *et al.*	1986	70+	1288	7.0	2.4

mild dementia is especially problematic. At what point does mildly forgetful behaviour become dementia? How do researchers allow for differences in intellectual abilities between the varying members of their study population? The issue of intellectual ability is especially important when considering the prevalence of mild dementia.

The type of instrument used to survey the population may well influence the resultant prevalence estimate. There has, however, been little work explicitly comparing the different instruments for identifying dementia. Recently Black *et al.* (1990) compared the information/orientation CAPE sub-test with a standard clinical interview and other dementia measures in a non-random sample of those aged 75 +. The impetus for this work was the seemingly low prevalence rates generated by the Melton Mowbray study. The comparative study illustrated the variability of the instruments. As might be expected the agreement was greatest for the unambiguous cases of severe dementia and diminished as the diagnosis became less clear cut.

Other factors concerned with study design will influence the degree to which prevalence rates may be compared across studies. These have been summarized by Henderson and Kay (1984) as follows:

1 Sample size. Large samples should permit more accurate estimates of prevalence than smaller studies. The number of subjects in the studies shown in Table 5.3 ranges from 300 to 1200.
2 Sample composition. Some studies include only those resident in the community while others also include the institutionalized population. Although the number of older people living in institutions is small the prevalence of dementia among this population appears to be high (see below). Their inclusion in a community prevalence study would therefore inflate the resultant prevalence rate.
3 The definition of the study population. As Table 5.3 shows there is a diversity between studies in the age taken as defining the elderly population. Some studies use the age of 65 + to define the elderly while others use age 70 +. Simple comparisons of prevalence estimates across studies is, therefore, problematic.
4 The age range within the study population. The age range of the study population will enormously influence the final estimated prevalence rate. This is because the prevalence of dementia seems to increase with age (see below). Inclusion in the study population of the young elderly (i.e. those aged 65–74) will deflate the rate for the group as a whole. Inclusion of large numbers of very old elderly in the study population will produce the opposite effect. Ideally all studies should produce age specific rates to overcome this problem. However the calculation of such rates is not legitimate if the sample size is insufficient.
5 Non-response bias. Published studies of dementia prevalence record non-response rates ranging from 8.7 per cent (Gruer 1975) to 20.3 per cent (Broe

et al. 1976). High rates of non-response may make the prevalence estimates invalid. We might speculate that those with dementia would be less willing to participate in a research project than the mentally fit. In addition, failure by respondents to complete all the items, known as item non-response, may also influence the result as those who do not complete the scale are excluded from the denominator.

Despite these methodological problems several commentators have attempted a synthesis of the results. Ineichen (1987) suggests an approximate dementia prevalence rate of 2.9 per cent of those aged 65 + while Brayne and Ames (1988) favour a rate of 5 per cent. However, these should be taken as approximate estimates. Given the observations about the importance of methodology, study design and case definition noted above we can probably conclude that there is no one single 'true' estimate of dementia. Rather there are a range of estimates resulting from the influence of study design factors and the reality that dementia is a continuous range of behaviours.

PREVALENCE OF DEMENTIA IN INSTITUTIONAL SETTINGS

The prevalence of dementia among those living in institutions appears to be high. However, there are a variety of different types of institutional setting in which an older person might reside. These are residential homes (either public or private), private nursing homes and long-stay hospital beds. Further details of the different types of residential care are contained in Chapter 7. Three of these studies suggest, for the institutional elderly population as a whole, a prevalence rate of approximately 30 per cent (Ames *et al.* 1988; Clarke *et al.* 1984; Mann *et al.* 1984). The more recent study in Belfast by Hodkinson *et al.* (1988) produced higher rates.

The institutional population varies considerably between these different care settings. Primrose and Capewell (1986) and Harrison *et al.* (1990) examined severe dementia prevalence in the different care settings. The latter study gave prevalence estimates of 44 per cent for local authority residential care, 63 per cent for long-stay hospital care and 32 per cent for private nursing homes. In long-stay psycho-geriatric beds the prevalence is virtually 100 per cent by definition! Support for the high prevalence of dementia in nursing homes is provided by Bond *et al.* (1989), in their study of the evaluation of NHS nursing homes; they reported that approximately 70 per cent of the nursing home population showed mild/severe dementia.

We may draw two main conclusions from these data about the prevalence of dementia among the institutionalized population. First, it is evident that rates are much higher in institutions as compared with community. This is not surprising as dementia is a major reason for admission to long-stay care. The second important point is that we must not treat the institutional population as a single group. Very broadly residential homes cater for the physically frail whereas nursing homes/long-stay hospital care is more likely to cater for the mentally frail. Consequently global prevalence estimates for the institutionalized elderly will underestimate the prevalence for hospital care and be an overestimate for the residential sector.

Prevalence rates relate to a specific point in time. This is why they are sometimes referred to as 'point prevalence'. It is difficult to use these data to draw any reliable inferences as to whether the prevalence among the institutional population is increasing.

INTERNATIONAL STUDIES OF DEMENTIA

International studies of dementia have all the above methodological problems combined with differences in the interpretation of behaviour which are culturally based. Gurland *et al*. (1983) undertook community surveys of the population aged 65 + in both London and New York. The study produced prevalence estimates of 4.9 per cent and 2.4 per cent respectively. Henderson (1990) suggests a prevalence rate for Japan of 4–6 per cent. More detailed work needs to be undertaken before it is possible to establish if there are geographical variations in the prevalence of this condition.

RISK FACTORS FOR DEMENTIA

Dementia is not a single disease; rather it is the manifestation of a number of different conditions. Establishing risk factors which identify those at an elevated risk of experiencing dementia is problematic because of multi-causality. It is probable that the risk factors for multi-infarct type are similar to those for stroke in which hypertension is implicated. To date there are few well established risk factors for dementia of the Alzheimers disease type. Other interesting hypotheses about potential risk factors for dementia include educational status, ethnicity, Downs Syndrome, aluminium and a wide variety of social and environmental factors.

DISTRIBUTION OF DEMENTIA WITHIN THE POPULATION AGED 65 +

The prevalence of dementia is not equally distributed between the different groups which comprise the post-retirement population. Although the precise rates vary, there is a clear trend for dementia prevalence to increase with age (see Figure 5.2). In the South Wales study described in the figure the prevalence of dementia ranged from 3 per cent of those aged 70–74 to 17 per cent of those aged 85 +. Morgan *et al*. (1987) report dementia prevalence rates of 1.8 per cent of those aged 65–74 and 5.6 per cent of those aged 75 +. From their comprehensive review Jorm *et al*. (1987) conclude that dementia prevalence increases exponentially with age with rates approximately doubling every 5.1 years.

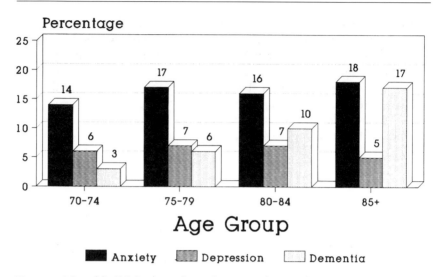

Fig. 5.2   Mental health by age of population aged 70+ in South Wales, 1980.
Source: Vetter *et al.* (1986).

Are women more likely to experience dementia than men? Both Copeland *et al.* (1987) and Morgan *et al.* (1987) publish data which indicates that dementia prevalence rates are higher among females than males (Table 5.4), as do Vetter *et al.* (1986) (see Figure 5.2). However, Jorm *et al.* (1987) concluded that there was no significant difference in overall dementia prevalence between the sexes; the increased rates among women were simply an artefact of the greater age of women studied. This review did suggest that the prevalence of Alzheimers disease was more common among women.

SURVIVAL OF THOSE WITH DEMENTIA

The study of the survival of those with a specific disease is important because survival rates combined with incidence rates determine the prevalence rate. Changes in mortality rates will result in either a decrease or increase in prevalence according to the direction of change in mortality. When considering survival rates three different starting points for the calculation may be identified; point of onset, point of diagnosis and point of entry into care. For the accurate calculation of survival rates point of disease onset is the theoretically most desirable starting point. However, the identification of the precise point at which any disease starts is problematic. This uncertainty is magnified when dealing with a disease like dementia where the onset may be highly insidious. Survival time from point of diagnosis is more easily determined but less useful. Disease diagnosis may vary both within and between communities because of

Table 5.4 Dementia prevalence by sex (%).

	Male	Female
Copeland *et al.**	2.7	6.8
Morgan *et al.**	1.6	4.4
Vetter *et al.***	5.0	8.0

*Population aged 65 +, **population aged 70 +.

differences in health care systems and structures. Consequently generalizations about survival after diagnosis may be problematic. Similarly, although survival from entry into care is easy to calculate, it is of little use as it is highly sensitive to the admissions policy of the institutions studied.

The relationship between dementia and mortality remains unclear. Several studies report increased rates of mortality among prevalent cases of dementia (Kay *et al.* 1970; Thompson and Eastwood 1981; Maule *et al.* 1984). A three-year follow up of a sample of elderly (aged 65 +) in Liverpool revealed that 44 per cent of women and 40 per cent of men defined as having organic brain disorders had died, compared with 11 per cent and 16 per cent of the well population. Jagger *et al.* (1989) report that, in a five-year follow up of the population aged 65 + in Leicestershire mortality rates of 87 per cent for the demented and 36 per cent for those without the condition.

Any change in the survival rate of those with dementia is of importance as this would influence the prevalence rate for the disease. Christie (1985), and Blessed and Wilson (1982), studying those admitted to hospital, suggested that survival after the diagnosis of dementia was increasing. A similar conclusion was reached by Gruenberg (1977) from a population study in Sweden, although further analysis of the same population failed to reach the same conclusion (Rorsman *et al.* 1986). While this is an important question because of its key impact upon prevalence rates, the survival time of those diagnosed as demented remains a subject of debate.

On the basis of the evidence surveyed it would seem that those with dementia do experience elevated mortality compared with their non-demented peers. However, it is unclear whether survival rates of those with dementia have increased or decreased over the post-war period. We may only speculate upon how these survival rates will change in future decades.

INCIDENCE OF DEMENTIA

There are far fewer studies of the incidence of dementia. Adelstein *et al.* (1968), using first contact with services to define the incident case, produced incidence rates of 1.9 and 2.1 per 1000 for those aged 60 +. Maule *et al.* (1984) report an annual incidence rate of 0.9 per cent of those aged 65 + in their Edinburgh study. Jagger *et al.* (1989), in a five-year follow up, report an annual dementia incidence rate of 1.4 per cent for the population aged 65 +. This study also produced annual age specific incidence estimates. These ranged from 0.9 per cent for those aged 75–79 to 2.56 per cent for those aged 85 +. Overall, Brayne and Ames (1988) suggest a guestimate annual incidence rate of 1 per cent for the population aged 65 +. However, much further work is required, especially in the calculation of age and sex specific rates. There is also considerable scope for more work examining, for example, differences between ethnic groups in terms of both incidence and prevalence in dementia.

HOW MANY CASES OF DEMENTIA WILL THERE BE IN THE FUTURE?

One of the main incentives for the collection of prevalence and incidence disease data is the identification of service needs for current and future generations. In future decades in Britain the relative number of elderly will increase. In addition, the very old will form an increasingly large element of the total elderly population. The broad implication of this demographic change is that those diseases particularly associated with the elderly will increase in prominence.

The most usual way of predicting future service needs is by the forward projection of current prevalence data to the predicted age structure of the population in the future. This method assumes both constant incidence and survival rates for the period of the population projections. This is the approach used by Ineichen (1987). Given our current state of knowledge about the dementing diseases we have few alternative options.

Ineichen (1987) suggests that future projections be based upon the forward projection of two rates: 1 per cent of those aged 65–74 and 10 per cent of those aged 75 +. In 1981 there were 5,200,000 people in Britain aged 65–74 and 3,300,000 aged 75 + (see Table 5.5). Applying Ineichen's prevalence rates to these populations suggests that there were 382,000 cases of dementia in 1981; by the year 2025 forward projection of these prevalence estimates would suggest that there will be 590,000 cases of dementia in Britain.

Table 5.5 Estimated number of cases of dementia in Great Britain, 1981–2025.

| | Population | | Cases of dementia | | |
	65–74	75 +	65–74	75 +	Total
1981	5,200,000	3,300,000	52,000	330,000	382,000
2025	6,000,000	5,300,000	60,000	530,000	590,000

Based upon suggested prevalence of 1% population aged 65–74 and 10% population aged 75 + (Ineichen (1987)).

Table 5.6   SAD scale.

(a) In the past month have you suffered from? If yes . . .
(b) Has it upset you a bit, a lot, or unbearably?

1 Frequent headaches (dummy item).
2 Worrying about every little thing.
3 A feeling of misery keeping you awake.
4 Breathlessness or pounding of the heart.
5 Depression without knowing why.
6 Being so 'worked up' you couldn't sit still.
7 Not caring if you woke up when you went to bed.
8 Feelings of panic without good reason.
9 Low spirits so that you sat for ages doing nothing.
10 A pain or tense feeling in the neck or head.
11 Feeling that the future is hopeless.
12 Worries keeping you awake at night.
13 A loss of interest in just about everything.
14 Anxiety so that you couldn't make up your mind on the simplest things.
15 Being so depressed that you thought about doing away with yourself.

Depressive illness

The main focus of work concerned with mental health in later life has been upon dementia; there has been much less empirical study of the affective disorders, depression and anxiety. 'Depressed' is a word frequently used, by both professionals and lay people, to describe an individual's mental state. Defining rigorously what constitutes a clinically significant depressive illness is problematic, regardless of the age range under consideration. In psychiatric terms depression is a broad concept which includes slowness of thought, negative thoughts, morbid sadness and depressed moods. Like dementia depression is obviously a continuum; where the case definition boundary is drawn will obviously influence the prevalence and incidence rates generated.

There are a number of different scales available to determine the prevalence of depression within different populations. One of the most popular scales is the symptoms of anxiety and depression (SAD) developed by Bedford *et al.* (1976) from the delusions, symptoms and states inventory (Foulds and Bedford 1979). The scale has been further developed for use with the elderly by McNab and Phillip (1980). Several community studies, most notably the ones in Nottingham (Morgan *et al.* 1987) and South Wales (Vetter *et al.* 1986) have used this instrument.

This scale consists of seven items relating to depression and seven to anxiety in the previous month (see Table 5.6). This scale is used in two stages. First subjects are asked if they have experienced each symptom. Those who respond yes are then asked if this has upset them 'a bit', 'a lot' or 'unbearably'. For each

88 HEALTH AND HEALTH CARE IN LATER LIFE

Table 5.7   Main British studies of depression.

Author	Age group	Sample	Prevalence rate (%)
Gurland et al. 1983	65+	396	12.4 (pervasive depression)
Copeland et al. (1987)	65+	1070	11.3
Morgan et al. (1987)	65+	1042	9.8
Vetter et al. (1986)	70+	1288	5.9

question a score of 0 to 3 is possible and the depression scale has a range of 0–21. A score of 6 is taken as indicating severe distress and 4–5 as borderline. A similar scoring system is used for the anxiety component.

As with dementia, different studies have produced a range of depression prevalence estimates ranging from 6 per cent to 12 per cent. These differences reflect the effects of the same set of research methodology factors as discussed for dementia. Overall it seems likely that about 10 per cent of the population aged 65+ experiences depressive illness of clinical significance (Table 5.7).

There is little evidence that the prevalence rate is age-related (see Figure 5.2). In South Wales 6 per cent of those aged 70–74 were defined as depressed compared with 5 per cent of those aged 85+. Morgan et al. (1987) report rates of depressive illness of 10.0 per cent for those aged 65–74 and 9.5 per cent for those aged 75+. Using a stricter definition of a case of depression produced only a small difference in depression prevalence between these two age groups (4.5 per cent and 5.5 per cent respectively).

A consistent finding of studies of depression is that rates for women are approximately double that for males of similar groups (see Figure 5.3). In the Liverpool study the depression prevalence for women was 13.6 per cent and 7.6 per cent for men (Copeland et al. 1987). Similar results have also been produced by Griffiths et al. (1987). One explanation for this gender differential in the prevalence of depression might be the greater percentage of elderly women who live alone.

Although the actual rates produced by studies appear to differ two trends seem to be consistent: the lack of an association between depression prevalence and age and an excess prevalence among women compared with men. This later sex difference in dementia prevalence is characteristic of the pre-retirement age groups. What are the causes of depression among older people? Murphy (1982) reviewed 100 cases and concluded that depression among older people had similar causes as for younger people and was focused upon major life events such as bereavement.

The prevalence of depression among the elderly in institutions has been less well researched. Mann et al. (1984) reported that the prevalence of dementia amongst assessable residents in the twelve homes studied was 38 per cent. Harrison et al. (1990) report depression prevalences among assessable residents

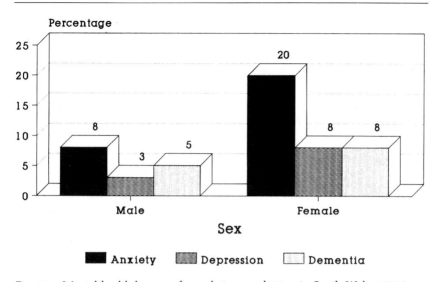

Fig. 5.3 Mental health by sex of population aged 70 + in South Wales, 1980.
Source: Vetter *et al.* (1986).

of 11 per cent in NHS long-stay psychiatric beds, 28 per cent for local authority residential homes and 35 per cent in private homes.

Cross-national studies of depression are both rare and difficult to interpret. However, the study of London and New York undertaken by Gurland *et al.* (1983) and using an explicitly comparable methodology produced rates of depressive illness of 12.4 per cent and 13 per cent respectively.

Anxiety

Another aspect of mental illness examined in community samples of the elderly is anxiety states. The SAD described above includes seven items concerned with anxiety (see Table 5.6). The scoring system is the same as described for depression.

Vetter *et al.* (1986) report that 15 per cent of those aged 70 + living in two areas of South Wales displayed symptoms of anxiety. This compares with the 11 per cent for the population aged 65 + reported by Morgan *et al.* (1987). There appears to be little change in prevalence rates with age (see Figure 5.2), but rates are considerably higher in women as compared with men (see Figure 5.3). The prevalence of this dimension of psychiatric disturbance in institutions has not been reported.

Table 5.8   Prevalence of malaise symptoms in last month (%), in Great Britain, 1984–85.

	65–74		75+	
	M	*F*	*M*	*F*
Difficulty sleeping	22	42	26	40
Always feeling tired	15	25	23	28
Worrying over every little thing	10	30	15	25
Nerves	6	17	7	15
Difficulty concentrating	10	17	14	17
Often or always bored	4	6	2	6
Often or always lonely	9	12	13	15
Often or always under strain	8	12	14	17
N	448	592	231	344

Source: Cox *et al.* (1987), Table 7.2.

Psychiatric symptoms

Further data concerning the prevalence of a variety of psychiatric symptoms are available from the health and lifestyle survey. The General Health Questionnaire (GHQ) is a 30-item psychiatric screening instrument which collects data about symptoms in the previous few weeks. A score of 4/5 is usually suggested as being indicative of psychiatric disturbance. Using this cut-off point the health and lifestyle survey reported that 27 per cent of men and 33 per cent of women aged 18 + could be classed as having psychiatric problems. This again serves to highlight the importance of the cut-off point in determining estimates of illness prevalence. There is little evidence from the GHQ that the percentage of the population scoring over these thresholds increase significantly with age. Of the 65–74 age group 25 per cent of men and 33 per cent of women scored 5 +; for those aged 75 + the respective percentages were 39 per cent and 43 per cent. The same survey developed a malaise index which is a simplified version of the GHQ. However, unlike the GHQ, it has not been validated against psychiatric opinion. This scale provides little evidence of increased rates of psycho-social disturbance among the older age groups (see Table 5.8). A higher prevalence of these symptoms among women as compared with men is obvious.

The relationship between mental and physical health

It is well documented that physical and mental health are inter-related. Vetter *et al.* (1986) demonstrates a consistent relationship between symptoms of anxiety and depression and physical disability. For example, 3 per cent of those without any physical disability showed symptoms of depression compared with 20 per

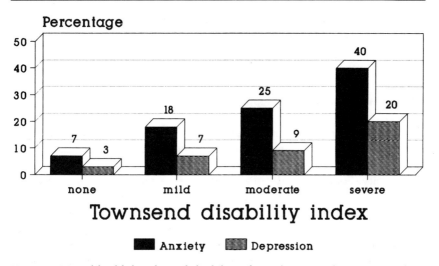

Percentage

Townsend disability index

■ Anxiety ▨ Depression

Fig. 5.4 Mental health by physical disability of population aged 70+ in South Wales, 1980.
Source: Vetter *et al.* (1986).

cent of the severely disabled; similarly 7 per cent of those without physical disability are defined as showing anxiety compared with 40 per cent of the severely disabled (Figure 5.4). Dementia prevalence is higher among those who are physically disabled. However, this relationship is confounded by the effect of age; disability increases with age, as does dementia. It is not yet clear if there is an independent relationship between physical health status and dementia.

No independent relationship has been established between hearing loss in later life and the three main components of mental health, anxiety, depression or dementia (Jones *et al.* 1984). However, visual impairment does seem to be related to both anxiety and depression. Jones *et al.* (1987) report that 36 per cent of those with some or much difficulty with sight are classed as anxious compared to 14 per cent without sight difficulties. For depression the respective percentages are 15 per cent compared with 7 per cent.

Social class and mental health

Little attention has been given to the relationship between mental and social class for the older age groups. Analysis of the data collected in South Wales revealed that there was no statistically significant difference in the prevalence of dementia or depression across the social class groups. However, the prevalence of anxiety was related to class: 9 per cent of those from social classes 1 and 2 were defined as anxious compared with 19 per cent from classes 4 and 5 (Victor

1989b). What this difference means is not clear; it could be a manifestation of a variety of factors including the very different financial circumstances of the two groups!

Mental health and social support

The importance of social support and contact for the health and well-being of individuals is well documented. The Alameda County longitudinal study reported higher mortality rates among those who were lacking in ties with the community. Social support remains, however, a rather nebulous concept to define and measure in social surveys. It may be defined objectively in terms of numbers of contacts between individuals. Alternatively, subjective feelings of the amount of social support may be important. Social support may be measured in terms of quantity or quality of contacts. Data from the health and lifestyle survey suggest that, regardless of age, symptoms of psycho-social disturbance are correlated with social support. Those with well defined social support networks illustrate lower rates of psychological disturbance than their more isolated counterparts.

Although this is a well identified relationship it is not possible to state the nature of the relationship. Are individuals psychologically disturbed because they are isolated or are they isolated because they are in some way disturbed?

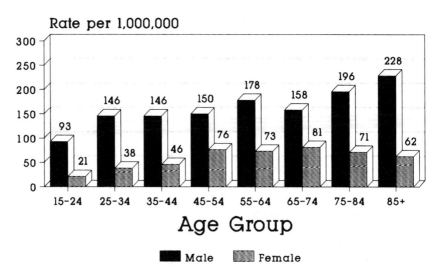

Fig. 5.5   Suicide rates in England and Wales, 1987.
Source: OPCS (1989b).

Suicide

Although suicide is not, in itself, a psychiatric illness it may be taken as suggestive of impaired mental health. In 1987 there were 3,986 cases of suicide in England and Wales. This is, almost certainly, a gross underestimate of the true number of suicides. Those aged 65 + accounted for 902 (23 per cent) of these recorded suicides. For men, the suicide rate increases with age; consequently the highest rate is illustrated by those aged 85 + , a rate of 228 per million population (Figure 5.5). At all ages rates for men are considerably higher than those for women of the same age. However, it is impossible to determine how this pattern is influenced by the known under-reporting of suicides.

Other mental health issues

Few studies have considered the prevalence of conditions such as mania and schizophrenia amongst the older age groups. For these serious psychiatric conditions the onset of new cases in later life appears to be very rare. Rather these are mental health problems which predate the onset of later life.

Conclusion

Our knowledge about mental health in later life remains patchy and is, in many domains, highly limited. Most data are derived from cross-sectional studies, with their inherent methodological limitations. Two types of mental health problem in later life may be distinguished: conditions identified in all age groups and those specific to the elderly. Affective conditions such as depression do not seem to increase with age. It appears that for these types of conditions few new cases are identified in later life. However, dementia is seen as being specific to the elderly age groups. Current evidence suggests that the prevalence of this disorder is about 1 per cent for the population aged 65–74 and 10 per cent for those aged 75 + .

One of the main reasons for the identification of the number of elderly (or any other age group) suffering from any disease is to establish information for service delivery and the planning of future services. Given the ageing of the population considerable interest has been expressed in identifying the number of elderly in the future who will experience this condition. This is usually undertaken by applying current global prevalence rates to projected future population structures. This method assumes, of course, that there is no change in either incidence or survival rates. Consequently all predictions of the number of future cases of a disease which are based upon prevalence rates will provide only approximate indications of future demands. For useful planning more accurate age specific incidence rate data are required.

6 HEALTH BELIEFS AND BEHAVIOUR

As indicated earlier the most persistent of all stereotypes about ageing is that the later phases of the life cycle are a time of universal, and inevitable, biological decline. This results in older people being consistently represented as ridden by physical and mental ill health. To be old is to be unhealthy. This perspective is not confined to Britain; it is found in many countries, both developed and less developed. Estes and Binney (1988, p. 69) describe the image of older people in America as 'to be old is to be frail, sick, dependent and vulnerable'.

The pervasiveness of this stereotype, especially in Britain, is probably the result of the interplay between several factors. Gerontological research has been heavily influenced by medical and biological theories which stress decline and sickness. Much research has started from the premise that old age is a social problem and has concentrated upon the problem dimensions of ageing such as ill health, disability and senile dementia, rather than examining normal ageing. Consequently in Britain there is a strong tradition of investigating the prevalence of ill health and specific medical conditions among older people. One consequence of this approach is that there has been comparatively little research examining the beliefs and attitudes of older people about their health. In a similar fashion investigation of health-related lifestyle behaviours in later life has also been neglected. In this chapter we examine aspects of the health beliefs and behaviours of older people.

What is health?

Health is a term which is used extensively but remains one of the most difficult ideas to define with any degree of precision. Indeed, health is a complex and multi-faceted entity which often defies the best efforts of researchers either to define or measure. One way of thinking about health is as the absence of disease. Disease is an easier concept to define as it is, in theory at least, identifiable by either deviation from measurable biological standards or by the presence of pathology. It is, however, not very easy to undertake population or community studies of disease for reasons of practicality. However, the concept of disease is not as clear cut as the above definition implies. The definition of what constitutes a 'disease state' is influenced by social concepts as is the definition of what is normal or average. Health is a much broader and socially defined concept than the simple absence of disease. As the classic WHO definition indicates, health is 'a state of complete physical, social and mental well being, not merely the absence of disease'.

It is, therefore, hardly surprising that the attitudes and beliefs held about health by the population and its constituent subgroups are both complex and superficially inconsistent. Studies in several areas of Britain have indicated that ideas about the meaning and definition of health held by the general population are complex (Blaxter 1983; Pill and Stott 1982, 1985; Williams 1983, 1990). These studies have indicated that health, for the lay population, seems to have three distinct dimensions: the absence of disease, as a functional concept (i.e. the ability to cope with daily activities) and health as a positive notion embracing ideas about fitness and general well-being. These ideas about the different aspects of health have been identified in a study undertaken in France (Herzlich 1973). It remains unclear as to how culturally and temporally specific these ideas about the main dimensions of health are.

There is a further complication in that individuals hold views about health at a variety of different levels of analysis. Strongly held beliefs at the individual level may not be maintained when describing health at the societal level and vice versa. Consequently both perspectives need to be examined when considering what people understand and mean by terms such as health.

GENERAL BELIEFS ABOUT HEALTH

It is difficult to investigate general beliefs about health within the confines of a large-scale structured survey. However, the health and lifestyle study, a large survey of a random sample of the British population carried out in 1984/85, offers insights into several aspects of beliefs about health and illness. One way of considering broad based beliefs about health was to ask, 'Are people more healthy now than in their parents' time?' The majority, 78 per cent of males and 75 per cent of females aged 65 +, thought that people were healthier than in their parents' time. This was little different from the responses provided by younger age groups. It might be expected that the percentage thinking that health had improved since their parents' time would increase with age. In fact the reverse pattern was observed. The proportion reporting that they thought people were healthier now than in their parents' time decreased with age, from 78 per cent of those aged 65–74 years to 67 per cent of those aged 85 years and over (Victor 1990a). There were no obvious gender or class differences in responses to this rather general perspective upon health in society.

Increased prosperity, improved diet and improved health services were the main factors advanced for improvements in health by the older age groups

Table 6.1 'Why are people healthier now than in your parents' time?' (%), in Great Britain, 1984.

	18–59	65–74	75+
Medical advances and improved availability	37	38	36
Health education	20	11	8
Improved living standards	21	31	33
Better environment	4	1	4
Better hygiene	4	4	4
Better working conditions	9	10	11
Better diet	40	38	36
More exercise	10	8	8
N	5554	1040	575

Source: Health and Lifestyle Survey (1987) – own analysis of unpublished data.

(Table 6.1). These responses, like those in the next sections, were provided by respondents without prompting and were classified at the data analysis stage of the study. Compared with younger age groups, older people are much more likely to suggest that improved prosperity has brought about improved health, while younger people are more convinced of the importance of health education. From these data older people seem to be identifying the importance of structural variables (e.g. income, living standards, etc.) in improving health status. In contrast the younger members of the population appear to be offering more individual behavioural dimensions to explain improved health status.

This difference between these rather broad age groups may be indicative of significant age-related variations within the population in terms of how they consider health. It seems unlikely that these differences are the result of ageing; rather they probably illustrate the effect of historical time and the differing general, social and cultural attitudes towards the cause of health and illness at varying points in time in Britain. If there are important differences in how varying generations perceive and conceptualize health then this has important implications for the development of health promotion and education strategies.

Concepts describing health

One way of investigating lay beliefs about health is to ask what attributes identify a healthy person. Respondents in the health and lifestyle survey were asked 'Think of someone who is very healthy, who are you thinking of and why do you call them healthy?' One interesting finding of this exercise was that for each age group the age of the healthy person approximated to the individual's broad cohort group. Across the age groups the healthy person was usually described as a male even when the respondent answering the question was female. Regardless of age health appears to be an attribute which is primarily associated with males.

When describing health in someone else three main themes are identifiable from the responses provided by respondents: health as a state of positive fitness; health as a state of not being ill; and health as being funtionally active. These models of health vary across the age groups (see Table 6.2). Younger people are more likely to identify health as being physically active or as the absence of symptoms (i.e. never being ill) than older people. Older people are more likely to represent health as a state of social functioning, such as being active. For example, 32 per cent of the pre-retirement age group see health as being physically fit compared with 10 per cent of the over-65 age group. Older people are also much more likely to describe health within the context of an individual's age. Older people, not unreasonably, relate health to others of their own approximate age rather than comparing themselves with younger people in their physical prime.

When describing what health means to them personally a different set of explanatory frameworks appear to be invoked (Table 6.2). Regardless of age and gender, health is viewed by the majority as a psychological rather than physical or social paradigm. Health is described by phrases such as being happy, being unstressed and being able to cope. Older people were much more likely than the young to be unable to describe what they meant by health. Underlying this broad level of agreement across the generations there are several significant age variations within the elderly population. With increased age there is a significant decrease in the percentage describing health as being physically fit from 13 per cent (65–74) to 3 per cent (aged 85 +).

Do men and women hold different views about what constitutes health? For those aged over 65 the responses were remarkably similar for both males and females. Both sexes are characterized by the predominance of the psychological definition of health at the individual level. Blaxter (1990, p. 30) gives some examples of the kinds of responses provided by respondents which fell into this psychological category. A 72-year-old female replied 'I think health is when

Table 6.2   Concepts used to describe health in Great Britain, 1984–85.

	In someone else			For self		
	18–59	65–74	75+	18–59	65–74	75+
Never ill	41	37	31	13	13	15
Physically fit	32	10	9	28	13	3
Active	15	22	20	19	28	31
Good habits	22	14	10	—	—	—
Psychology	9	10	8	59	57	48
Appearance	—	5	4	—	—	—
Healthy for age	5	17	17	—	—	—
Can't explain	—	—	—	7	9	12
N	6654	1040	575	6654	1040	575

Source: HLS (1987) – own analysis of unpublished data.

you feel happy. Because I know when I feel happy I feel quite well', while a 74-year-old farmer's widow stated 'I've reached the stage now where I say isn't it lovely and good to be alive, seeing all the lovely leaves on the trees, it's wonderful to be alive and to able to stand and stare!'.

Perceptions of health status

One aspect of health status omitted from the previous chapter on morbidity relates to perceived health status. This is concerned with how people evaluate their overall health status. Typical of such questions is, 'Compared with other people of your age how do you rate your health in the last year?'. Clearly there are problems in interpreting responses to these types of questions. It could be argued that such questions are of little value as respondents may be unwilling to label themselves as being in poor health. Nor do we know what comparative standards our informants are using. There have been a large number of studies which have sought to establish the validity and accuracy of replies to this sort of question. Responses to this question correlate well with consultation with a GP, mortality and adjustment to illness (Blaxter 1990). However, the question is included in the analysis presented here as a broad overall indicator of how older people feel about their general health status.

The General Household Survey asks respondents to rate their overall health as good, poor or fairly good for the previous year. Overall 40 per cent of those

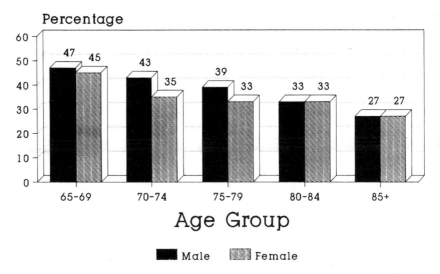

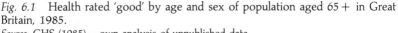

Fig. 6.1 Health rated 'good' by age and sex of population aged 65 + in Great Britain, 1985.
Source: GHS (1985) – own analysis of unpublished data.

aged 65 + rate their health as good. Women are less optimistic about their health status than men: 38 per cent of women aged 65 + rate their health as good compared with 44 per cent of men. There is a decrease with age in the percentage describing their health as good and a rise in the percentage reporting poor health (Figure 6.1). For example, 46 per cent of those aged 65–69 report their health as good compared with 32 per cent of those aged 85 +. Although there is a marked decrease with age in the percentage rating their health as good this is not matched by an increase in the percentage classed as poor. Approximately 21 per cent of men and 25 per cent of women in each group define their health as poor. The decrease in the percentage classed as good is matched by an increase in the percentage defined as fairly good. So with increased age there is a switching of health rating from good to fairly good but no large increase in the percentage classing themselves as in poor health.

The relationship between health rating and gender is rather more complex than the overall rating described above might indicate (Figure 6.1). Between the ages of 65 and 79 men are more optimistic about their health rating than women. However, over the age of 80 years there is little difference between the sexes.

In the previous two chapters we have shown that there are marked social class variations in the health status of older people. Consistently those older people from professional and managerial occupations experience better health than their contemporaries from the manual occupation groups. Is this pattern illustrated for overall health rating? Scrutiny of Figure 6.2 indicates that this

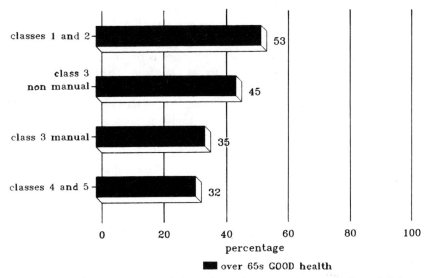

Fig. 6.2 Health ratings by social class of population aged 65 + in Great Britain, 1985.
Source: GHS (1985) – own analysis of unpublished data.

Table 6.3 The relationship between health rating and chronic and acute health problems, in population aged 65 + in Great Britain, 1985.

| | | Health rating | |
	Good	Fairly good	Poor
Chronic health problem	34	69	90
Acute health problem	5	15	41
N	1829	1220	1076

Source: GHS (1985) – own analysis of unpublished data.

pattern is replicated for overall health rating. Of those from social classes 1 and 2 53 per cent rated their health as good, compared with 32 per cent from classes 4 and 5.

As with aspects of physical and mental health the population classification derived from overall health ratings is dependent upon the question asked. If a health status question asks people to rate their health in comparison to others of their own age the pattern of age-related change in responses does not materialize. Consistently, approximately 60 per cent of the population aged 65 + rate their health as good, 30 per cent as fair and 10 per cent as poor (Victor 1987). How well does older people's overall rating of their health status compare with the prevalence of acute and chronic health problems? There is a strong correlation between those who rate their health as poor and the prevalence of chronic health problems (see Table 6.3). Hence 90 per cent of those who rate their overall health as poor also report chronic health problems, compared with 34 per cent of those who report good health. The relationship is less obvious for acute health problems.

Asking hypothetical or speculative questions is one way of investigating perceptions and feelings about certain issues. Data from the health and lifestyle survey (Cox *et al.* 1987) suggest that older people are fairly negative about future health status. Almost a quarter (22 per cent of those aged 65–74 and 23 per cent aged 75 +) consider that it is very likely that someone of their age will develop a serious illness over the next ten years. Only 4 per cent and 7 per cent respectively rate this prospect very unlikely. However, it is not obvious whether the respondents expect this to happen to them specifically or if it is a population level observation.

Healthy lifestyles in later life

Health behaviour is concerned with the strategies and responses to illness demonstrated by individuals as well as the activities undertaken to preserve, promote and maintain health. This includes activities undertaken by individuals to prevent disease or to detect it in an asymptomatic state. The health maintaining and promoting activities of older people have been neglected, although their importance has been recognized by WHO when it stated that '... Health education, information on the promotion of health and prevention of disease' was required for the older age groups (WHO 1982, p. 8). Health behaviour in later life is clearly rooted in the social context in which older people live and reflects the influence of such activities at earlier phases in the life cycle. We may further distinguish between preventive and health maintaining behaviour. Preventive behaviour describes those activities designed to reduce the risk of developing an illness, while maintenance describes activities designed to maintain and, perhaps, improve health. The potential range of preventive and maintenance activities among older people is clearly substantial, ranging from smoking cessation to ensuring that a dwelling is adequately heated.

Aspects of individual lifestyle, as well as structural factors, are related to health. Much of the current climate of education about health stresses the importance of individual lifestyle behaviours. Lifestyle is a term which is often used but very rarely defined. Implicitly it is conceptualized in terms of the personal behaviours which individuals indulge and which are well recognized as risk factors for various diseases. Increasingly attention is paid to the four lifestyle areas of smoking, alcohol consumption, exercise and diet. How do older people fare with regard to these aspects of health related behaviour?

HEALTHY BEHAVIOUR

Overall, the vast majority of the older age groups, 91 per cent of those aged 65–74 and 88 per cent of those aged 75 +, felt they were leading a fairly or very healthy life. Only 1 per cent felt that they were leading a very unhealthy lifestyle (Table 6.4). What features made their lifestyle healthy? Three factors dominate the leading of a perceived healthy life: taking exercise, having a good diet and being of moderate habits (Table 6.5). Interestingly non-smoking and non-drinking were cited by many fewer respondents as contributing to being healthy.

Table 6.4 'Do you feel that you lead ...?' (%), in population aged 65 + in Great Britain, 1984–85.

	65–74	75 +
Very healthy life	26	28
Fairly healthy life	65	60
Not very healthy life	7	7
Unhealthy life	1	2
Don't know	1	3
N	1040	575

Source: HLS (1987) – own analysis of unpublished data.

Table 6.5 'What makes your life healthy?' (%), in population aged 65 + in Great Britain, 1984–85.

	65–74	75+
Taking exercise	28	23
Good diet	24	32
Of moderate habits	20	21
Feeling fit	19	15
Fresh air	15	14
Don't smoke	11	9
Don't drink	9	8
N	852	506

Percentage does not total 100 as multiple responses allowed.
Source: HLS (1987) – own analysis of unpublished data.

Table 6.6 'What are the three most important things you do to keep healthy?' (%), in population aged 65 + in Great Britain, 1984–85.

	65–74	75+
Walking	42	36
Diet	29	22
Gardening	23	25
Leisure activities	17	13
Fresh air	11	10
Housework	10	18
Stop/reduce smoking	4	1
Stop/reduce drinking	3	2
N	685	348

Source: HLS (1987) – own analysis of unpublished data.

The health and lifestyle survey reported that overall about 70 per cent of the British population reported that they 'did things' to promote their health. This proportion showed remarkably little variation with age. Two types of behaviour, diet and exercise, dominated the activities proposed as the health promoting behaviour in which older people participated in (Table 6.6). In terms of exercise older people were more likely to report activity such as gardening while younger subjects suggested active sports. There is considerable interest among older people in doing (more) things to promote their own health. This is perhaps in sharp contradiction to the common stereotype of older people passively accepting the onset of the tide of ill health associated with later life. Increased exercise/activity was the health promoting/improving activity which the majority of older people wanting to improve their health suggested (Table 6.7). This was the option preferred by 50 per cent. If these responses are extrapolated to the general population aged 65 + then there is a massive unmet

Table 6.7 'Are there things you would like to do to keep yourself healthy?' (%), in population aged 65 + in Great Britain, 1984–85.

	65–74	75 +
Yes	38	34

If yes – what would you like to do? (%)		
	65–74	75 +
Sport/exercise	66	50
Diet/nutrition	3	2
Lose weight	5	4
Give up/cut down smoking	6	4
Give up/cut down drinking	1	—
Pursue hobbies	7	10
Change social life	5	5
N	394	196

Up to three responses allowed.
Source: HLS (1987) – own analysis of unpublished data.

demand among the older age groups for improved access to leisure facilities. It is, perhaps, salutary to reflect upon how difficult we make it for older people to use the range of leisure facilities provided either because of physical access problems, inappropriate classes and high entry costs.

LIFESTYLE FACTORS

Four lifestyle factors – smoking, alcohol consumption, exercise and diet/weight control – are well established risk factors for a variety of diseases. How well do older people perform on these key behavioural factors?

Smoking

Smoking, of either cigarettes, pipes or cigars, is not equally distributed throughout the population. The prevalence of smoking varies within the population in terms of factors such as age, gender, social class and ethnicity. The lowest rates of smoking are found among the population aged 60 and over (see Table 6.8). For men the older age groups also contain the highest proportions of ex-regular smokers. The data describing the prevalence of smoking illustrates a good example of a cohort effect as older women, those aged 60 and over, have the highest proportions classed as never smoking. This reflects the influence of cultural and social factors as it was totally unacceptable for women to smoke when these women were in their formative years in the interwar period. Smoking for women became socially acceptable only in the 1939–45 war and after. This is now being reflected in the high rates of lung cancer and heart disease among women.

Table 6.8   Prevalence of smoking (%), in population aged 60+ in Great Britain, 1984–85.

	Current		Ex-smoker		Never smoked	
	M	F	M	F	M	F
60–69	44	30	41	26	13	44
70–79	41	18	46	25	12	57
80+	26	8	58	20	17	71
All 18+	47	32	27	20	25	46

Source: Cox *et al.* (1987). Table 10.1

Epidemiological studies have consistently pointed to the health hazards associated with smoking, but most studies have looked at health risks amongst those who are middle aged. However, Kaplan *et al.* (1989) examined the impact of smoking status on mortality over a 17-year period for 60- to 94-year-olds included in the Alameda County study in the United States. The results indicated that current smokers showed excess mortality when compared with non-smokers. Those who gave smoking up in later life occupy an intermediate position. The evidence now suggests that giving up smoking in the seventh decade of life brings health benefits. Active steps should be taken to encourage older people to quit smoking (Vetter *et al.* 1988).

Alcohol consumption

The pattern of alcohol consumption among the older age groups is very similar to that for smoking. Older people are less likely to consume alcoholic drinks than the younger age groups and those who do drink consume less than their younger contemporaries. Overall 22 per cent of men aged 60+ and 54 per cent of women are non-drinkers or have never drunk alcohol (see Table 6.9). This compares with 8 per cent and 23 per cent respectively for the 18–39 year age group. Again several factors explain this distribution: the higher mortality of very heavy drinkers; the influence of social attitudes; the fact that when the older age groups grew up attitudes against drink and for temperance were very much stronger; and possibly the fact that the reduced incomes of older people offer less opportunity to consume alcohol (there is a clear relationship between alcohol consumption and disposable income).

Diet

Dietary habits cover a range of areas including frequency and regularity of eating, the type of meals consumed and the regularity with which certain types of food such as fruit are eaten. Clearly researching these areas is highly problematic, especially if details about the amount of food eaten are required. The health and lifestyle survey has investigated some of these aspects.

Table 6.9   Prevalence of alcohol consumption (%), in population aged 18+ in Great Britain, 1984–85.

	Non-drinker		Occasional		Regular	
	M	F	M	F	M	F
18–39	5	8	7	20	88	72
40–59	6	12	12	22	82	66
60+	11	22	21	34	68	44
all 18+	6	12	11	24	87	64

Source: Blaxter (1990), Table 6.4.

However, it is very difficult to devise a scale which summarizes dietary habits on a range from good to bad. Older people are more likely to eat breakfast than other age groups; conversely they are less likely to eat snacks or have meals outside the house. This reflects a variety of influences. Traditional wisdom bases 'a good diet' around the consumption of three meals a day of which breakfast is seen as the most important. Older people are more likely to eat red meat and less likely to eat fruit, vegetables and salad. However, it is difficult to identify if this reflects a cohort effect: does this reflect what this age group were brought up to believe was a healthy diet or the reduced income of older people?

Exercise

Exercise is now seen as being an important aspect of lifestyle which is associated with health status. A sedentary lifestyle is now seen as being a very important risk factor for heart disease and other conditions. Few older people, approximately 10–20 per cent, participate in active leisure pursuits such as swimming or jogging. However, participation in activities such as gardening and walking is high among these age groups, as we saw earlier. The benefits of activity in promoting good psychological and physical health among older people are increasingly being recognized. Data from North America indicate that the mortality risk of those who remain active in later life is lower than their more sedentary counterparts (Kaplan and Haan 1989). It would seem that there is considerable evidence for increasing the participation of older people in such activities as swimming.

Weight control

It is also suggested that, in the interests of health, we should maintain our weight within desirable limits. One method of calculating desirable is the body mass index (BMI). This expresses weight in kilograms divided by height in metres squared (W/H^2). Using data from the health and lifestyle survey shows

Table 6.10 Distribution of body mass index by age and sex (%), in population aged 60+ in Great Britain, 1984–85.

| | 60–69 | | 70–79 | | 80+ | | All ages | |
	M	F	M	F	M	F	M	F
Underweight	4	4	8	4	20	7	8	4
Acceptable	38	36	49	32	33	38	49	50
Overweight	48	40	37	45	41	32	36	31
Obese	10	21	7	19	6	23	8	15

	Male	Female
Underweight = BMI	< 20	< 18.6
Acceptable = BMI	20.1–25.0	18.7–23.8
Overweight = BMI	25.1–29.9	23.9–28.5
Obese = BMI	> 30	> 28.6

Source: Cox *et al.* (1987), Table 4.3.

that a lower proportion of the older age groups have a BMI within what is defined as indicating a correct weight (see Table 6.10).

Policy implications

Elucidating lay beliefs concerning health is of considerable policy importance. It is vital to consider what, if any, differences there are between lay and professional concepts about health. Successful health education/promotion should be grounded in a strong understanding of how people conceptualize their own health. Health campaigns based upon an inadequate understanding of the health beliefs held by the target population stand little chance of success.

Compared with those aged under 65, the post-retirement age groups are more likely to consider that health has improved since their parents' time. This is, perhaps, not surprising as, over the lifetime of the current cohort of older people, there have been very substantial improvements in the health of the British population. Older people identify improvements in material circumstances such as housing, diet and general prosperity, and improved and more widely available health care, as the reason for improved health. In contrast the younger members of the sample were more likely to favour health education/promotion as the reason for improved health. This might suggest that older people hold a more collectivist public health notion of improving health status. It may also suggest that older people are more fatalistic about their health. From a health promotion perspective it would seem that individualistic based exhortations to improve health will have little chance of success amongst the older age groups. Two strategies are worth pursuing. First, older people could be made more aware of the importance of changes in individual behaviour and their potential health benefits. Implicit within this strategy is the promotion of a positive view of health. Second, health campaigns for this age group appear to stand more chance of success if promoted at a group/societal level.

Older people have, until recently, been largely excluded from health education/promotion activities. This reflected a very negative and ageist view that there was little which could be done to improve the health of older people. This view no longer holds sway and health educators/promoters are increasingly turning their attention to older age groups. However, before any such activities can be successful it is imporatnt to understand how older people conceptualize their health. Programmes may then be designed which build upon these notions. As yet, however, we cannot be certain about the most effective route by which these activities can have maximum impact within the older age groups. However, Barnard (1988) argues that the empowerment of the older age groups is essential to this process. Furthermore, improved material circumstances for most older people are a prerequisite; no amount of activity will promote changes in behaviour and attitudes if the target group has inadequate material resources with which to change their lifestyle.

7 HEALTH CARE PROVISION AND USE

Health and social care for older people are provided by the formal sector (i.e. agencies of the state such as hospitals) and the informal network of family and friends. This chapter examines the contribution of the health care agencies. In considering the health care provision agencies we may usefully divide them into two main types: primary care and secondary care.

The structure of health care provision

As was briefly described in the introduction, Britain has a socialized system of health care which is largely funded from general taxation. The NHS aims to provide a comprehensive range of care which is free at the point of consumption. The objective of the NHS is the provision of an equitable health care service which is accessible to all citizens of Britain regardless of where they live or of their financial and personal circumstances. The pre-April 1991 organization of the NHS distinguishes between DHA-run services and primary care. DHA services include acute and long-stay hospital care, psychiatric hospital provision and community nursing services, including health visiting. These services are run and managed by the DHA. Primary care is used to define the family doctor service. Under the arrangements for health care provision current in 1990 the DHA was not responsible for the provision of general practitioner (GP) services. Within the National Health Service the general practitioners (GPs) are independent contractors.

THE PRIVATE MEDICAL SECTOR

The medical profession were reluctant to accept the creation of the NHS and to obtain their agreement to the creation of the service they were allowed to retain their private practices. Consequently throughout its existence the NHS has been complemented by a residual system of private provision. Doyal (1979) reports that only 3 per cent of consultants work entirely in the private sector.

The continued existence of the private sector has allowed those with sufficient resources to avoid the worst aspects of the state system.

The provision of private medicine, both within and without the NHS, has remained a controversial issue. Governments of varying political persuasions have attempted to either decrease or increase the role of the private sector. The Conservative government elected at the 1979 and two subsequent elections has sought to encourage the development of a system of private medical care alongside the NHS. This development has been proposed as a way of improving standards in the NHS by stimulating competition. One method of paying for private health care is via insurance. Several firms such as BUPA specialize in this aspect of health insurance. Currently 8 per cent of the population has private health insurance, which is usually paid for by an employer rather than by the individual. Private health insurance coverage rates vary within the population from 10 per cent of those aged 45–64 to 4 per cent of those aged 65 +. The leading companies are reluctant to provide insurance for this age group and those who will include older people in their schemes have very high premiums.

The private sector does not aim to produce a comprehensive system of health care; in Britain it has developed specialized aspects of health care provision. Ham (1985) reports that the private sector provides 5 per cent of acute beds, 8 per cent of all beds and receives about 8 per cent of all non-emergency admissions to acute hospitals. The private sector makes a major contribution in the field of elective surgery such as hip replacements and is now also a significant provider of long-term care for the elderly via the development of private residential and nursing homes (see Chapter 8).

CHANGING THE STRUCTURE OF HEALTH CARE PROVISION: THE NHS REVIEW

Many of the proposals contained in the White Paper *Working for Patients* (DOH 1989a) have passed into law as a result of the British Parliament passing the NHS and Community Care Bill in June 1990. The proposals, in force from April 1991, contained in this document are consistent with the ideology of the administration in that it is an attempt to apply market principles to the institution which is the cornerstone of the British welfare state.

The detailed proposals were noted in the introduction. However, at the heart of the changes is the creation, within the NHS, of an internal health care market. This is to be achieved by the separation between those who will be responsible for purchasing care (DHAs and budget holding GPs) and the providers of care (i.e. opted out NHS hospital trusts, the independent sector and directly managed NHS hospitals) (see Figure 7.1). The theory underpinning this reorganization is that competition between providing units will increase both the range and quality of the services provided. The DHA (or other purchasing agent) will then, it is argued, be able to obtain care for their residents which

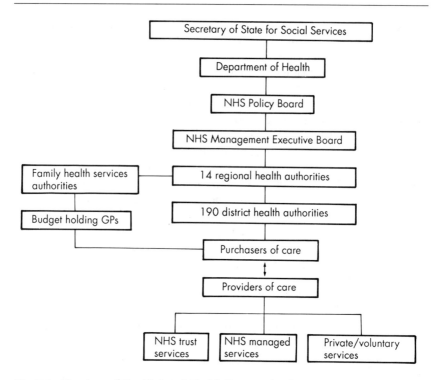

Fig. 7.1   Structure of the National Health Service, April 1991.

provides greater value for money. This, of course, relies very heavily upon being able to define and measure value for money.

SPECIALIST HEALTH CARE PROVISION FOR OLDER PEOPLE

Pre-NHS voluntary hospitals were reluctant to accept patients who were chronically ill. Consequently the NHS inherited a large number of public hospitals containing many who were defined as chronically ill and written off as being impossible to rehabilitate and restore to the community or independent living. A disproportionate number of these patients were elderly. The post-war period in Britain has been characterized by the development of geriatric medicine as a legitimate medical specialism. This branch of medicine owes much to the pioneering efforts of Marjorie Warren who demonstrated that, with proper assessment and rehabilitation, many of the elderly in these chronic sick establishments could be returned to independent living. However, it should be noted at this stage that only a minority of elderly patients are treated by the geriatric services.

The definition of geriatric medicine proposed by the British Geriatrics

Society (BGS) is 'the branch of medicine concerned with the clinical, preventive, remedial and social aspects of illness in the elderly'. However, the BGS declines to offer a definitive identification of 'the elderly'. Very broadly this speciality is concerned with the treatment of acute episodes of illness, the management of long-term health problems and with those who are admitted to long-stay beds in hospitals. Key features of geriatrics as a medical specialism are the concepts of assessment and rehabilitation, a concern with multi-disciplinary working and the recognition of the importance of social factors in disease onset and management.

No agreed definition of who is a geriatric patient has yet been arrived at. Here we may draw an analology between geriatrics and paediatrics, another age-based medical specialism. Paediatrics has, given the declining birth-rate, been extending the upper age range of its client group, while geriatric medicine has been extending the minimum age of its client group. As we will see later, people aged 65 + are the main client of the NHS. If the age of 65 + was adopted as the definition of geriatrics then the NHS should be renamed the National Geriatric Medicine Service.

The way in which specialist health services for the elderly are provided nationally varies considerably. Some areas operate an age-related service whereby all medical admissions above a certain age, usually 75 +, are seen by the geriatricians. In other areas geriatrics patients are defined by their need for rehabilitation and multi-disciplinary care. So although in Britain we have a national system of health care provision the way services have developed shows considerable variation between districts. One feature which appears central to both versions of geriatric provision is the commitment to the provision of a service which is area-, rather than simply hospital-, based. Hence domiciliary visits by medical staff are an integral part of any specialist service. How such patterns of provision will be influenced by the imposition of the market discipline remains the subject of considerable discussion.

How much is spent on health care services?

Having considered the structure of health care provision in Britain we next consider how much is spent on the provision of these services. Expenditure on the health service is a significant item within the national budget, representing about 5 per cent of gross domestic product (Table 7.1). There are extensive debates about whether this percentage of GDP is, in fact, adequate. Clearly Britain spends a lower percentage of its GDP on health care than other countries. For example, Sweden and France spend just over 9 per cent of GDP on health care, while the United States spends 11–12 per cent of GDP on health care (Leathard 1990). It is not as clear, however, how much more Britain 'ought' to spend on health care, although many commentators are agreed that the present amount is insufficient.

Table 7.1 Estimated programme budget for health care services in £ millions in England, 1986–87.

Programme	£ million	% of total on aged 65+
Acute in-patients	3519.2	45.8
Acute out-patients	1134.5	19.1
Obstetric in-patients	431.9	—
Obstetric out-patients	81.3	—
Geriatric in-patients	902.4	97.6
Young disabled	23.0	1
Geriatric out-patients	8.1	100
Mental handicap in-/out-patients	496.6	16.2
Mental illness in-patients	998.2	57
Mental illness out-patients	71.4	57
Non-psychiatric day patients	66.8	76.1
Psychiatric day patients	79.6	57
Other hospital	633.8	34.8
Health visiting	164.3	9.9
District nursing	331.6	74.6
Chiropody	34.5	89.7
Other community	4328.2	46.2
Total	10317.2	48.4

Source: Bosanquet and Gray (1989), Table 26.

How is the health care budget distributed? Leaving aside debates about the adequacy of the overall budget we can also consider how the current budget is distributed. There are four main ways of considering this question:

1 Between geographical regions.
2 Between different arms of the health care system (e.g. hospital versus community services).
3 Between varying client groups (e.g. paediatrics versus psychiatry).
4 Between varying age groups.

It is well documented that there are geographical variations in both health status and health care expenditure within Britain. A special committee, the resource allocation working party (RAWP), was convened to establish ways of moving towards a fairer distribution system. It might be naively assumed that these variations in expenditure reflect the varying patterns of need for health care illustrated by the population. No such correlation is evident. Indeed, the available evidence supports the opposite conclusion: expenditure is greatest in areas of least need and lowest in areas of greatest need. Observation of this pattern led to Julian Tudor-Hart (1971) formulating his 'inverse care law' which he stated as '... the availability of good medical care tends to vary inversely with the need of the population served'.

If we examine expenditure by type of care provided, i.e. hospital or community, then it is obvious that acute in-patient care dominates the programme budget, accounting for 34 per cent of all expenditure. It has been the policy of successive governments since 1976 to move the balance of expenditure from hospital to community services. However, this redistribution has not yet taken place to any significant extent, with the acute hospital sector managing to preserve its stranglehold upon health care expenditure.

A third way of considering expenditure distribution is via the allocation given to specific patient or client groups. Scrutiny of Table 7.1 reveals that hospital and maternity services account for the majority of funds. The so-called Cinderella specialisms of mental health, mental handicap, the physically disabled, and specialist services for the elderly are less well resourced. The final perspective upon resource allocation is by age group. It is the very oldest age group, those aged over 85, who record the highest per capita expenditure at £1452 per person per annum (Table 7.2). Clearly in simple population terms the older age groups account for a disproportionate amount of health care expenditure. For example, those aged 85 + represent 1 per cent of total population and account for 8 per cent of health care expenditure. Those aged 65 + account for 48 per cent of all NHS expenditure, as compared with 20 per cent in 1951/52 (Bosanquet and Gray 1989). This increased expenditure upon the older age groups probably arises from the inter-relationship of several factors including: price inflation in health care; population change; the increased use of health services.

Although we can look at expenditure patterns in a number of different ways three main points are evident. First, any attempts at reducing expenditure on the NHS will impact most significantly upon the older groups, who are the main consumers of health care services. Second, the increase in the numbers of very elderly will, if current trends persist, impose considerable extra demands upon the health care system. Simply to maintain current patterns of expenditure will require considerable expansion of the budget, without allowing for techno-

Table 7.2 NHS estimated annual expenditure per head by age group in England, 1986–87.

Age group	Expenditure per head (£)	% total expenditure
All births	1184.0	7.3
0–4	196.6	5.8
5–15	97.2	6.3
16–44	83.2	16.4
45–64	160.5	16.1
65–74	414.8	17.0
75–84	926.9	22.7
85 +	1452.3	8.6

Source: Bosanquet and Gray (1989), Tables 27 and 28.

logical changes in service provision. Third, the NHS changes are very concerned with improved management and 'efficiency' and do not seem to confront the need to increase resources simply in order to maintain the status quo.

Utilization of hospital services

Acute non-psychiatric hospitals play a vital role in the provision of medical care for all members of the community but especially older people. At its creation the NHS inherited the existing stock of hospital provision. This varied widely in both the quantity and quality of the fabric and type of buildings. At the time of its creation the NHS took over about 1700 public hospitals and about 1000 voluntary hospitals, a large proportion of which were facing bankruptcy. To overcome the piecemeal pattern of provision which was the legacy of the pre-NHS supply the 1960s saw the policy of developing a network of district General Hospitals. These were acute hospitals providing a full range of services to a population of about 100,000–150,000. There was a clear acceptance of the need to plan acute hospital provision in order to equalize the distribution of hospital beds throughout the country and replace much of the existing pre-First World War hospital stock. The philosophy of planning services centrally in order to achieve equitable distribution has clearly been abandoned by the new NHS philosophy which concentrates upon local decision making and competition rather than cooperation between hospitals.

HOSPITAL UTILIZATION BY OLDER PEOPLE

Annually about 9 per cent of the population visit hospital as an in-patient. The percentage of the population reporting a hospital in-patient stay shows a J-shaped distribution very similar to the pattern for mortality (see Figure 7.2). For the older age groups men have a higher rate of hospital admission than women. For those aged 75 and over 20 per cent of men and 16 per cent of women reported an in-patient stay in hospital in the previous year.

Levels of in-patient hospital admission in Britain are lower than those reported from North America. Mullner et al. (1987) report that 20 per cent of Americans aged 65 and over were admitted to hospital in 1986; this represents 10.8 million hospital admissions. In Britain 11 per cent of those aged 65 + are admitted to hospital annually, approximately half the American rate. It remains a subject of debate as to whether this enormous difference in admission rates reflects differences in morbidity (i.e. demand for care) between these two countries or differences in the supply of hospital beds.

HAVE HOSPITAL UTILIZATION RATES CHANGED OVER TIME?

Data about utilization of hospital services over time are sparse. One source for considering if utilization rates are increasing (or decreasing) is via the

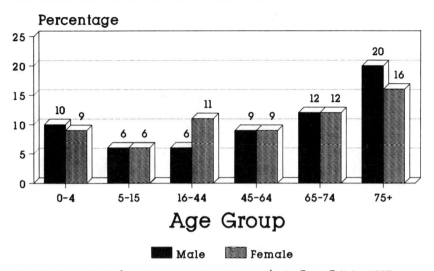

Fig. 7.2   In-patient admissions in previous 12 months in Great Britain, 1987.
Source: OPCS (1988b).

comparison of hospital discharge rates based upon information from the hospital in-patient enquiry (HIPE). Unfortunately information is available about discharges rather than admissions. Further, these data are flawed for detailed examination in that they do not distinguish between those discharged dead and those discharged alive! Using these data to inform decision making about the quality of care offered by different hospitals would obviously be problematic.

A pattern of increasing acute hospital utilization is observed if we compare age specific hospital discharge rates for the period 1979 to 1985 (Figure 7.3). Overall discharge rates increased by 25 per cent between 1971 and 1985 from 856 per 10,000 population to 1074 per 10,000. For those aged 65–74 hospital discharge rates increased by 35.8 per cent between 1971 and 1985 – an annual average increase of 2.2 per cent. For those aged 75 + the increase in discharges was 46 per cent over the same period (average annual increase of 2.7 per cent) (Bosanquet and Gray 1979).

Why have discharge rates increased? These data reflect, to some degree at least, activity within the hospital sector. Clearly there appears to have been a significant increase in activity across all age groups, but especially among the older age groups. Whether these increases reflect increased morbidity, a greater willingness to care for older people or an expansion in capacity is a matter of debate.

HOW DO OLDER PEOPLE ENTER THE HOSPITAL SYSTEM?

There are a variety of different ways in which an individual may access the hospital system and end up as an in-patient. Very broadly these are as an

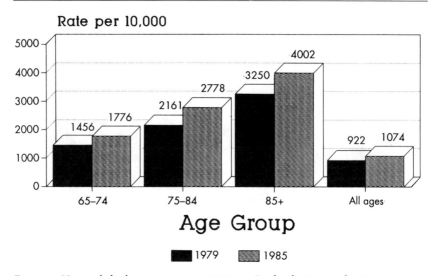

Rate per 10,000

Fig. 7.3 Hospital discharge rates per 10,000 in England, 1979 and 1985.
Source: Bosanquet and Gray (1989).

emergency, via a GP referral, from an out-patient clinic or via a waiting list. Under the current system of provision, waiting lists, usually for elective surgery, are one way of rationing health care. The issue of the length of waiting lists, their variation in length between areas and the amount of time an individual patient may wait remain highly contentious. Reducing waiting lists is at the top of all politicians' political agendas, regardless of their political persuasion.

About 20 per cent of admissions of those aged 65 + are via the waiting list. The vast majority of older people enter hospital as a result of an emergency or medical referral. This raises several issues. Are clinicians reluctant to put older people on surgical waiting lists because they are in some way discriminating against older people? Are the kinds of medical problems faced by older people more likely to present as an emergency than those posed by younger age groups? Is the debate about reducing waiting lists less relevant to the medical care needs of older people than the younger age groups? Is an obsession with reduced waiting lists an example of covert ageism?

It is likely that the creation of the internal market, if it does emerge, will be heavily concentrated towards elective surgical procedures. The idea of travelling between areas to take advantage of shorter waiting times appears to have some public support as Leathard (1990) quotes a survey which suggests that 40 per cent of people would go anywhere in the country to avoid waiting for treatment. However, it is unclear if older people, who are least likely to have access to transport, are in favour of this idea. Again, a concentration upon elective surgical procedures may mean a reduced provision of other acute services, to the detriment of the older age groups.

TREATMENT SPECIALISM

Hospital medicine is a highly specialized activity. This is reflected in the way care is provided. Upon entry to hospital older people will be admitted to the branch of medicine dealing with their type of illness. For example, an older person with a fractured femur or requiring a hip replacement will be cared for by an orthopaedic surgeon; someone requiring a cateract operation will be under the care of an ophthalmologist.

In what medical specialisms are older people treated? Data from HIPE give some indication of where in the hospital service older people are treated. Overall those aged 65 + represent 33 per cent of all discharges from hospital; if paediatric and obstetric beds are excluded then those aged 65 + account for 60 per cent of discharges. Those aged 65 + are, therefore, the largest single consumer group of the services provided by acute hospitals. The older age groups are, by definition, the main clients of the geriatricians. However, they also form the largest single patient group for general medicine (44 per cent), general surgery (32 per cent), ophthalmology (49 per cent) and orthopaedics (27 per cent).

Older people are not confined, when cared for in an acute hospital, to the geriatrics department; they are the single largest patient group for most major medical specialisms. When considering how demographic change may affect the demand and supply of health care it is important to remember that such changes in demand will affect all the major medical specialisms and not be confined to departments dealing exclusively with older people.

The appearance of older people as the largest single patient group in most major medical specialisms is a fact which is not yet recognized by the training offered to medical and nursing staff. Given the distribution of older people throughout the different medical specialisms it could be argued that all doctors (and nurses) should receive some training in the main aspects of geriatric medicine, with its emphasis upon rehabilitation and the role of multi-disciplinary care and assessment. Data from a study in Wales suggested that patients treated by geriatricians were more likely to receive post-discharge services than their contemporaries treated by general physicians (Victor and Vetter 1985b).

LENGTH OF STAY IN HOSPITAL

How long do older people remain in hospital? The average length of stay in hospital for older people is usually longer than that for a young person with a similar medical condition. This reflects the multiple pathology which is often a feature of older people presenting with specific medical conditions. Average length of stay increases with age from 14 days for a person aged 65–74 to 34 days for someone aged 85 + (Figure 7.4). Length of stay also varies between different medical specialisms. For example, the average duration of stay in general medicine for a patient aged 65–74 was 14 days compared with 17 days

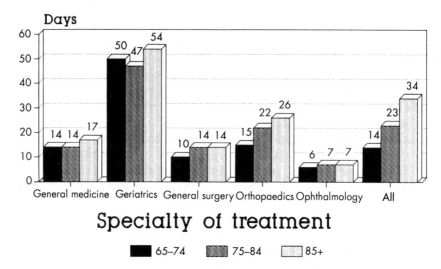

Specialty of treatment

■ 65–74   ▨ 75–84   ☐ 85+

Fig. 7.4   Average length of stay by age and specialism in England, 1985.
Source: OPCS (1987).

for a patient aged 85 +. This difference is hardly surprising as treatment specialism is acting here as a proxy measure of morbidity.

One of the most characteristic features of the hospital sector in Britain in the past decade has been the massive overall reduction in the average length of stay (Table 7.3). The largest overall reductions have been achieved in the 85 + age group. Between 1981 and 1986 the average hospital stay for a patient aged 85 and over decreased by 7.7 days. The specialisms of geriatrics and orthopaedic surgery have recorded the largest decreases in average length of stay. Taking a longer timespan, 1971–85, Bosanquet and Gray (1989) report that the average stay for a patient aged 65–74 decreased by 34.8 per cent from 22.1 days to 14.4 days. For a patient aged 75 + the decrease was from 41.4 days to 24.7 days, a decrease of 40.3 per cent.

These trends for a reduction in length of stay are not unique to the older age groups. Between 1971 and 1985 average duration of stay for all age groups decreased from 15.1 days to 10.7 days, a decline of 29.1 per cent. Nor are these trends unique to the British system of socialized medicine. In the United States average stay for a patient aged 65 + decreased from 13 days in 1967 to 8.8 days in 1986 (Eisdorfer *et al.* 1987).

TRANSFER FROM HOSPITAL BACK TO THE COMMUNITY

For many patients, irrespective of age, admission to an acute hospital constitutes only one phase of their medical career. Many patients need continuing care, follow up or rehabilitation. It is a strong commitment to the concept of continuing care in the community which is a hallmark of the approach and philosophy of geriatric medicine. A constant theme in research concerned with the hospital care of older people is the discharge from hospital back to the community. Discharge is, perhaps, the wrong term to use. This implies a severing of relationships when many older people will need continuing care; perhaps the term 'transfer' would be more appropriate.

Research has consistently demonstrated that the transfer of older clients from hospital to the community can be very problematic with older people being sent home without adequate arrangements having been made for their continuing care (Victor 1983). Some medical specialisms, especially geriatric medicine, are much better than others at arranging effective transfer. This problem centres upon effective communication between hospital, community and local authority services. Despite the regular production of research reports arguing for better discharge planning little seems to have changed, especially in specialisms other than geriatric medicine.

The issue of an effective and humane transfer of an older person from hospital to the community is of considerable importance. In order to effect such a transfer a whole variety of different agencies may be involved including remedial therapists, GPs, social work, community nursing and domiciliary services. Under our current system of care provision there are problems in co-ordinating the activities of these different agencies. It is unclear as to how proposed changes in the systems of NHS and social care provision will improve communications between agencies. One example of how there may be problems with the new system is the case of stroke. The care of stroke patients involves a plethora of different health and social care workers. When DHAs are looking to purchase stroke care how many different contracts will they have to place? Will they have to contract for rehabilitation services separate from the contract for acute beds? How will follow up and rehabilitation services for patients who have undergone joint replacements be organized if the surgical contract has been placed with a hospital some distance away from the DHA? The introduction of markets and contracts is obviously going to be fraught with problems for those patient groups who present a multiplicity of different health and social care needs.

Table 7.3 Change in length of stay by age and specialism (days) in England, 1981–86.

	65–74	75–84	85+
General medicine	−1.5	−2.0	−5.0
Geriatrics	−9.4	−14.6	−16.1
General surgery	−1.3	−1.5	−2.1
Trauma and orthopaedics	−3.0	−3.6	−5.1
Ophthalmology	−1.6	−2.5	−2.2
All	−2.2	−4.7	−7.7

Source: OPCS (1987).

READMISSIONS TO HOSPITAL

These significant reductions in the duration of hospital episodes for older people have prompted the suggestion that this may have an adverse effect by increasing readmissions rates. The scenario depicted is that decreased hospital stay means that older people (or indeed patients of any age) are being sent home with high levels of dependency; community services/informal carers cannot cope and the person has to come back into hospital. How accurate is this stereotype?

It is problematic trying to consider hospital readmission rates as most hospital computer systems currently in operation are not easy to interrogate and rarely produce information about readmissions on a routine basis. Consequently specially designed research projects have attempted to enumerate hospital readmission rates. Typical of such studies was a project undertaken in Parkside DHA, an Inner London health district (Victor and Jefferies 1990). This study followed up a cohort of 386 patients aged 65 + for six months after their discharge home. At the end of the study period 130 (38 per cent) had been readmitted to hospital within Parkside; 68 (18 per cent) were readmitted within one month and 25 (6 per cent) were readmitted within seven days of their initial admission. The number of readmissions ranged from 1 to 16.

The above study is subject to several of the methodological and conceptual problems which surround attempts to quantify readmission rates. First, there is no accepted definition of the time period for which readmissions should be calculated. Second, there are problems surrounding the ability to capture admissions to hospital. The Parkside study relied upon readmissions which occurred within the three hospitals within the DHA and underestimates readmission rates as it excludes readmissions which happened outside the study area. Third, studies cannot accurately quantify mortality rates. It is highly probable that many of those in the initial cohort of patients would have died. These limitations serve to underestimate readmission rates. Studies based in Britain on the 65 + age group have consistently failed to identify age or sex as 'risk' factors for readmission (Victor and Vetter 1985a; Graham and Livesley 1983; Andrews 1986). The data from Parkside conform with the results of previous British studies by failing to link readmission to the demographic characteristics of patients.

Readmission rates were related to initial length of stay. The average length of stay of readmitted patients was 12 days compared with 15 for those not readmitted. Patients readmitted consistently had a shorter length of stay in all specialisms than non-readmitted patients. This, at face value, at least supports the notion that short length of stay may be linked to subsequent readmission to hospital. However, much more work is required before it is possible to state if the relationship between these two events is causal.

MEASURING THE QUALITY OF HOSPITAL CARE: THE ROLE OF
READMISSION RATES

The debates about the relationship between length of stay and readmission
have served to highlight the potential of readmission rates being used as a
surrogate measure of outcome after hospital care. One feature of the debate
about the proposed changes in the structure of the NHS is an increased
emphasis upon the measurement of the quality of care provided by the different
elements of the health care service. Measuring the quality of the hospital service
is obviously difficult, especially given the diversity of different forms of
treatment. One measure which has been proposed as a quality of care indicator
is readmission to hospital. The simplistic assumption underlying this suggestion is that hospitals with high readmission rates are providing a poorer quality
of care than hospitals with lower readmission rates.

The use of readmission rates as an indicator of outcome rests upon the
assumption that they may be used as a proxy for morbidity resultant from poor
clinical care. The validity of this key assumption has not been proven.
Conceptually, all readmissions are bad, since to go into hospital again may be a
profoundly disturbing and negative experience for the patient (i.e. a poor
patient outcome). However, it is simplistic to assume all readmissions are
indicative of poor patient care as some readmissions are planned. Further it is
obvious that other factors such as the social circumstances of the patient, his or
her environment and the provision of care in the community by both formal and
informal carers are also important in influencing readmission.

Unplanned or emergency readmissions may be a more useful outcome
indicator. However, unplanned readmissions that are due to a new disease are
not necessarily suggestive of poor care. Thus, only those unplanned
readmissions in some way related to the index admission have any utility as a
surrogate measure of outcome. Further, such measures suggest notions of
avoidability. To develop a meaningful measure of readmission which has any
validity as a measure of clinical care requires that the admission be unplanned,
related to the index admission, and in some way avoidable. Operationally, this
might be defined as those unplanned readmissions occurring within a 'short'
(but specified) interval after the first discharge. The debate about using
readmission to measure quality of care is obviously much more complex than it
seems at first sight.

The recent Acheson Report on *Public Health in England* identified 'ensuring
the means to evaluate health services' as one of the three core tasks of the public
health function in the NHS. This emphasis upon evaluation has been reinforced
by the recent White Paper on the future of the NHS. The utility of using
readmissions as an index of outcome and as a surrogate method of identifying
'poor' clinical care is limited by the conceptual and methodological limitations
noted earlier. Readmission to hospital after an initial episode of treatment is not
solely dependent on the quality of the initial care but is dependent on a whole

variety of factors unrelated to the initial in-patient stay. Consequently readmission has little future as a general indicator of outcome, even though the increasing ease with which this index may be calculated by using computerized patient admission data bases is a strong attraction.

THE INAPPROPRIATE USE OF ACUTE BEDS BY OLDER PEOPLE

The most appropriate way of providing health care for older people within the hospital sector remains a point of contention. There are those for (Horrocks 1982) and against (Evans 1983) the establishment of age-related specialist services for elderly people. Although the merits of each approach have been described, no rigorous evaluations of these different perspectives on the care and treatment have been undertaken. However, even if an age-related service is established for those older people with acute medical problems, older people will remain high consumers of services provided in surgery and other specialist areas of modern medicine.

Alongside the debates about the most appropriate method of caring for the elderly are concerns about the 'blocking' of acute beds by older people who no longer need the facilities provided by an acute setting but who, for other reasons, cannot be discharged. It is a common stereotype that substantial numbers of acute hospital beds are occupied by older people who no longer need them. This then raises the question as to what is the inappropriate use of an acute hospital bed? How are the so-called bed-blockers to be identified? It is no surprise to realise that those studies which have investigated the problem of 'bed blocking' have concentrated upon older hospital patients; studies have not researched this topic for younger people as their right to an acute hospital bed appears to go unquestioned.

How is the bed-blocker to be identified? Simply asking staff to identify inappropriately placed patients is obviously potentially subject to bias from several sources. Previous research which has considered the problem of the blocking of acute beds by inappropriately located patients have related staff views to a length of stay for four weeks (or more) (Coid and Crome 1986). Using this protocol a survey of two Inner London hospitals revealed that of older patients (i.e. those aged 65 +) were classified as bed blockers (Victor, 1990b). This estimate suggests that 8 per cent of acute beds were being 'blocked' by these patients.

Patients likely to be labelled as bed blockers consistently display problems such as incontinence and dementia which are likely to present considerable nursing care problems (Victor 1990b). Why are such patients described as being inappropriately placed? Data from a study in Inner London revealed that the single most important reason cited was the need for nursing/institutional care (81 per cent). Comparatively few elderly were remaining in hospital because of community care/social problems.

The debate about the blocking of acute beds by elderly people is interesting for it calls into question how the health care needs of older people are evaluated. Furthermore, it is worth emphasizing that the blocking of beds by inappropriately placed patients is not a feature unique to the elderly. However, it is very rare indeed for the question about the inappropriate use of acute beds by younger patients to be raised. The whole notion of bed blocking seems to imply that older people enter hospital and then wilfully continue to occupy a bed which, in the views of staff, they no longer require. Older people (or indeed patients of any age) do not become bed blockers of their own intent. Rather where such cases do occur it is because the health and social care system cannot provide the type of care these patients need.

Hospital consumer satisfaction

What do older people think of hospital care? Little is known about the attitudes of older people towards the services offered by the acute hospital sector. A survey of the over 75s living in South Wales revealed that 86 per cent had either visited or stayed in a general hospital ward compared with 33 per cent for a geriatric ward (Salvage et al. 1988, 1989). Of those interviewed 52 per cent reported that they would be pleased to enter a general ward compared with 13 per cent for a geriatric ward and 10 per cent for a geriatric hospital. These negative perceptions of the geriatric ward/hospital confirm the findings of several other previous studies. The main advantages of all three settings related to the quality of care offered. However, the main perceived disadvantage of the general ward was the 'noise', which was mentioned by 23 per cent. The main disadvantage of the geriatric ward/hospital was 'being surrounded by ill elderly', which was cited by a third of respondents.

More data about general attitudes towards the health service is available from the British social attitudes survey (Table 7.4). The majority of people, regardless of age, were satisfied with the NHS as a whole. However, levels of overall satisfaction do seem to have dropped between 1983 and 1987. It is difficult to interpret this change in attitudes, which could reflect increased levels of patient expectation, a decrease in the quality of the service provided or a combination of the two. Levels of satisfaction with in-patient care are generally high. However, concerns are expressed about the waiting times for elective surgery and out-patients and a perceived need for more medical and nursing staff. Overall it appears that the very oldest age group, those aged 75+, express the least criticism of the services provided.

A part of the recent NHS White Paper was devoted to the need for hospitals to undertake much more extensive 'market research' in order to establish what the clients (patients?) wanted to be provided. However, they are given little guidance as to how they should go about undertaking such projects. Luck et al. (1988) report their experiences of undertaking market research in a variety of settings for South Birmingham DHA. Their study of quality of care for the

Table 7.4   Levels of satisfaction with the NHS (%) in Great Britain, 1983–87.

	NHS as a whole		In-patients		Out-patients	
	1983	*1987*	*1983*	*1987*	*1983*	*1987*
65–74	15	30	2	6	5	7
75 +	10	20	1	5	1	6
All ages	26	40	6	13	21	13

Views on needs for improvements in hospital services			
	65–74	*75 +*	*All*
Waiting time for elective surgery	80	77	87
Waiting time for out-patient appointments	74	69	83
Staffing by nurses in hospitals	65	49	75
Staffing by doctors in hospitals	64	47	70
Quality of hospital treatment	23	12	30
Quality of hospital nursing	15	7	21

Source: Bosanquet and Gray (1989), Tables 17 and 18.

elderly in hospital, with specific reference to respite care, is illustrative of these types of surveys. Patients and relatives responded more positively to the ward survey than did visitors. Does this reflect a real difference in perceptions or the reluctance of patients and their carers to criticize in case their respite care arrangements were jeopardized? All consumer surveys undertaken in hospital could be restricted in their utility because patients, in a dependent position, may be reluctant to offer their 'true feelings or observations'. The Birmingham study highlighted three problem areas: patient autonomy (i.e. wearing own clothes, deciding what time to get up); ward facilities and layout and communication between hospital staff and carers. The first issue requires a change in organization practice and attitudes towards the patient group. The second requires capital changes. Neither of these two problems will be easy to confront. If changes are not made as a result of these surveys then such enterprises may lose credibility and be seen as a diversionary tactic.

Utilization of mental hospital services

Separate information is available for utilization of mental hospital beds which distinguish between first admissions and all admissions. Those aged 65 + are significant users of mental hospital beds. In 1986 they accounted for 34 per cent of all admissions and 37 per cent of first admissions compared with 22 per cent and 27 per cent respectively in 1976 (DOH 1989c).

For both first and all admissions to mental hospitals the rate increases progressively with age (see Figures 7.5 and 7.6). There is a marked gender difference in first admission rates; the rates for women being approximately

Rate per 100,000

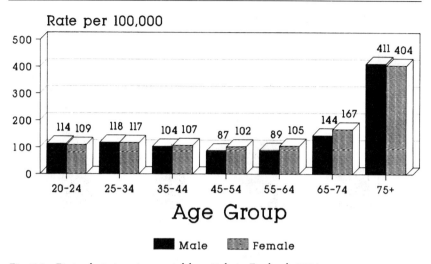

Fig. 7.5   First admissions to mental hospitals in England, 1986.
Source: Department of Health (1989c).

Rate per 100,000

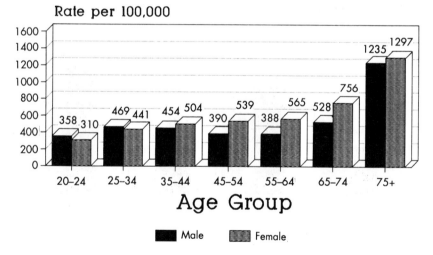

Fig. 7.6   All admissions to mental hospitals in England, 1986.
Source: Department of Health (1989c).

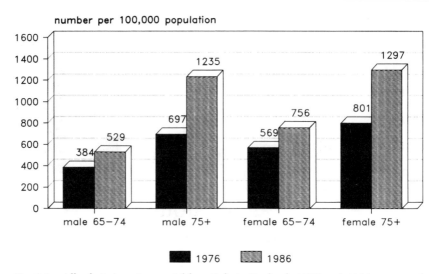

Fig. 7.7 All admissions to mental hospitals in England, 1976 and 1986.
Source: Department of Health (1989c).

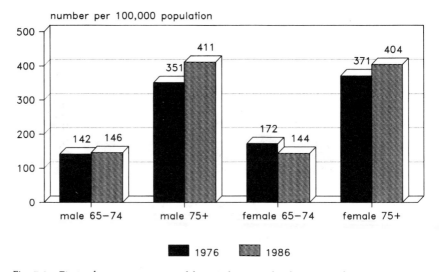

Fig. 7.8 First admissions to mental hospitals in England, 1976 and 1986.
Source: Department of Health (1989c).

one-third higher than for males. No such difference is observed for all admission rates.

As with the use of acute beds there has been a significant increase in utilisation by older people during the years 1976–86. In that ten-year period there was a slight decrease in overall first admission rates; − 4 per cent for males and − 16 per cent for females. For those aged 65 + only women aged 65–74 years show this decrease in first admission rates (see Figures 7.7 and 7.8). Over the same period overall mental hospital admission rates increased by 14 per cent for men and 5 per cent for women; the increases in admission rates characteristic of the population aged 65 + were considerably greater than this. For example hospital admission rates for men and women aged 75 + increased by at least 60 per cent during the decade.

Primary health care

In Britain every member of the population is registered with a doctor whose circumstances may range from working alone (a single-handed practice) to working within a large health centre consisting of several GPs working in concert. In the British system of socialized medicine consultation with a GP is free. It is now stated policy to encourage GPs to group together into health centre-based practices. However, this is not easy to achieve because, as was noted earlier, GPs are independent contractors and free to practise as they wish.

The role of the GP with older patients is, potentially, limitless. However, in a report on the potential contribution of family doctors to the care of older people Almind et al. (1983) proposed four key principles for good primary health care of older people. These were:

1 To help prevent unnecessary loss of function.
2 To prevent and treat health problems which adversely affect quality of life in old age.
3 To supplement the existing system of informal care and prevent its breakdown.
4 To give older people a good death as well as a good life.

GP CONSULTATION RATES

What percentage of the population consult their GP? According to the 1987 General Household Survey (GHS) 17 per cent of those aged 65–74 and 22 per cent of those aged 75 + consulted a GP in the 14 days before interview compared with 15 per cent for the general population (Figure 7.9). For both males and females there is a U-shaped pattern of consultations, with the highest rates being reported for the very young. Annually it is estimated that approximately 75 per cent of those aged 65 and over will visit their family

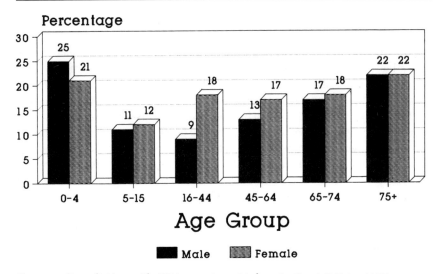

Fig. 7.9   Consultation with GP in previous 14 days in Great Britain, 1987.
Source: OPCS (1988b).

doctor. Millard (1988) estimates that on any day in 1981 the family doctor was caring for approximately 2 per cent of those aged 75 and over.

Establishing trends over time in GP consultation rates is problematic. Comparing 1972 and 1987 shows, for all age groups, a slight increase in GP consultation rates in the 14-day reference period (see Figure 7.10). At all ages consultation rates are higher among females as compared to males. However, the differences are quite slight in most age groups.

Where do older people see their GP?

Older people like other members of the population may consult their GP at the surgery or request a home visit. There is a clear trend for the number of older people reporting a home visit to increase with age from 18 per cent of those aged 65–69 to 62 per cent of those aged 85 + (Figure 7.11). Such visits are time consuming and may increase the GP's workload significantly. Consequently it is estimated that those aged 65 + account for 27 per cent of GPs' time in 1981/82 as compared with 22 per cent a decade earlier. If this pattern is maintained in the future then the increased number of those aged 85 + will have important implications for the workload of family doctors. We may speculate that GPs may become less willing to maintain the very elderly on their lists when they have to provide care within a specified cash-limited budget.

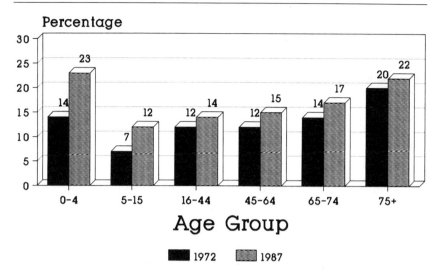

Fig. 7.10 Consultation with GP in previous 14 days in Great Britain, 1972–87.
Source: OPCS (1988b).

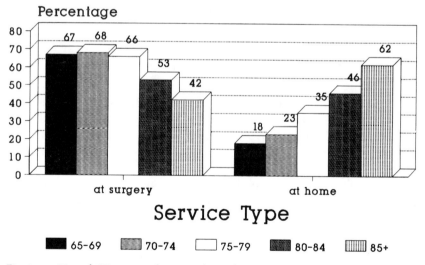

Fig. 7.11 Use of GP services by age of population aged 65 + in Great Britain, 1985.
Source: GHS (1985) – own analysis of unpublished data.

Table 7.5   Need for improvements in aspects of the GP service (%) in Great Britain, 1987.

	65–74	75+	All ages
GP appointment systems	31	28	47
Time per patient given by GP	21	19	33
Ability to choose GP	15	14	29
Quality of treatment by GP	18	10	26

Source: Bosanquet and Gray (1989), Table 19.

CONSUMER VIEWS ON THE GP SERVICE

What do older people think about the services offered by the GP? Data from the British social attitudes survey indicate that attitudes towards the service provided by GPs are very positive (Table 7.5). There are few who express complaints with the quality of care offered. However, there is some dissatisfaction with the system for providing care functions. Particular problems are centred around the time available for consultations and the workings of the appointment system. Few appear to express problems in the system of changing GPs. Yet making this easier is one of the changes enshrined in the NHS and Community Care Bill. How will this Bill affect what patients appear to want, longer consultations and improved appointment systems?

CHANGES IN PRIMARY CARE: THE IMPOSITION OF THE NEW GP CONTRACT

Following the White Paper *Promoting Better Health* (DHSS 1987) a new GP contract has been imposed upon family doctors by the Department of Health and came into force in April 1990. The stated objective of this new contract is to improve the standard of general practice and it proposes substantial changes in the way general practice is structured and financed. Included in the new contract is the compulsory retirement of doctors at the age of 70. One aspect of the contract which has provoked much discussion is the identification of specific activities which family doctors must undertake and the setting of targets for specific activities such as cervical smear testing.

   With regard to the health care of older people the most salient feature of the new contract is that they will be required to annually invite each patient on their list aged 75 and over to participate in a consultation which should assess the health of the patient. In return for undertaking this activity GPs will be rewarded with a special fee for each patient screened. The health check will cover six main dimensions: sensory functions, mobility, mental condition, physical condition including continence, social environment and use of medicines. The result of each assessment invitation must be recorded in the patient's notes. Clearly this is an attempt to impose a national screening and surveillance programme to monitor the health of older people. However, the GP may subcontract out the screening visits/consultations to other health professionals working under his or her direction.

SCREENING AND THE ELDERLY

This imposition of routine health screening for the older age groups in the new GP contract is obviously premised upon the assumption that routine screening is beneficial to the health of the population. However, this is a rather questionable assumption. The only British trial of health screening in the non-retired population failed to identify any positive health benefits in favour of the screened group.

For older people there have been a variety of different screening trials using an assortment of highly diverse methodologies. Postal screening (Barber and Wallis 1976) and visits from nurses (Tulloch and Moore 1979) and health visitors (Vetter et al. 1984; Luker 1988) have all been used as methods of routinely screening all the elderly in a given population.

What have the results of such projects been? All have identified considerable 'unmet' need for services in the populations screened. Routine visiting by a health visitor may increase the receipt of services by older people (Vetter et al. 1984). However, what are the health outcomes of offering such screening services? Vetter et al. (1984) in a study of elderly in South Wales, reported decreased mortality among their screened group of elderly. However, this study did not find any differences in morbidity between the two groups.

The alternative to universal screening is a more selective approach, focusing upon the high risk groups. This, of course, begs the question of who is in the high risk group. For older age groups the conventionally accepted high risk groups have been the very elderly (i.e. aged 85 +), the recently bereaved, those recently discharged from hospital, those living alone and those who have recently moved. However, Taylor et al. (1983) argue that only very advanced age and recently discharged from hospital actually warrent identification as indicators of vulnerability.

The mandatory imposition of this task upon GPs has generated an extensive debate about its efficacy. A survey of primary health care team workers in Bath DHA reported that 80 per cent favoured regular assessment of those aged 75 + in their own homes (Tremellan and Jones 1989). However, there was no clear agreement between the professions surveyed as to who should undertake these assessments, although 89 per cent felt that it should involve the health visitor. Those interviewed favoured a case finding approach rather than true screening, i.e. the identification of asymptomatic disease. Social, environmental and daily living activities were suggested as the appropriate basis for assessment rather than clinically based assessments and tests.

Although it is difficult to estimate what positive health benefits for the older person will result from the imposition of a national screening system there will be profound implications for the health and social services. Since the seminal paper by Williamson and colleagues (1964) every survey of the elderly at home has identified significant amounts of previously unmet need. These range from the need for hospital admission to the need for community support services such as chiropody. How such probably very extensive unmet need will be met without a substantial increase in resources remains to be seen. Indeed, is it ethical to undertake assessments if the GP cannot then deliver appropriate services to meet the identified needs?

Community nursing services

Community nursing services are funded and managed by the District Health Authority (DHA). Throughout this volume the term 'community nursing' is taken to include the work of district nurses of all grades ranging from auxiliary to sister/charge nurse and health visitors. Up until 1974 these services were organized by local authorities rather than health authorities. Consequently such services have only been under the administration of health authorities for a short while. Much of the pattern of provision of community nursing services and their mode of working reflects their origin as a non-health authority administered service. These nurses may work from a GP practice or DHA health clinic. Their work is primarily concerned with the care of patients and focuses upon technical procedures such as injections and dressings and the personal care of patients, e.g. bathing, etc. In contrast health visitors, who are also DHA funded, are concerned with prevention and assessment, especially in the field of child care and development. These services are usually geographically based and have a strong local connection.

In 1986 the Cumberlege Report proposed that district nurses, health visitors and school nurses should come within the umbrella term community nursing. This report proposed a change in the orientation of nursing services from hospital to the community. In summary the report proposed that nursing services should be organized around a target population of 10,000–25,000 within a geographically defined area. This concept is, however, rather difficult to implement as there is often no easily definable area around which to develop services. This problem is especially acute in urban areas where there is no co-terminosity between areas used to administer health, GP or social services. Furthermore, areas such as wards or enumeration districts used for the collection and analysis of census data are usually not related to administrative areas used by service providers. The future of these recommendations has been further confused by the changes contained in the recent NHS White Paper.

District nursing and, to a lesser degree, health visiting services are important for older people. Those aged 65 + represent about 50 per cent of the workload of district nurses and 10 per cent of health visitor workloads (Table 7.6). In 1985

Table 7.6 Role of community nursing staff with people aged 65 + in England.

	District nursing		Health visiting	
	1982	*1987/88*	*1982*	*1987/88*
Total treated (000)	3433.1	3459.6	3811.6	4093.0
% treated aged 65 +	43	47	12	10

Source: Department of Health (1989c), Tables 6.1 and 6.5.

approximately 5 per cent of those aged 65 + were in receipt of district nursing services and 4 per cent health visiting services, compared with 2 per cent for both types of service in 1972. Utilization rates for both these services increase significantly with the age of older people. For example, 2 per cent of those aged 65 to 69 are in receipt of district nursing care compared with 20 per cent of those aged 85 + (see Figure 7.12).

What do older people know about community nursing services? District nurses are well known. Salvage *et al.* (1988) report that 87 per cent of those aged 75 + were aware of the district nursing service as compared with only 20 per cent for the health visiting service. However, levels of satisfaction were high among those who had received either service.

While the proportion of the population aged 65 + receiving community nursing doubled between 1972 and 1985 the situation for health visiting remained constant. The role of health visitors with older people remains

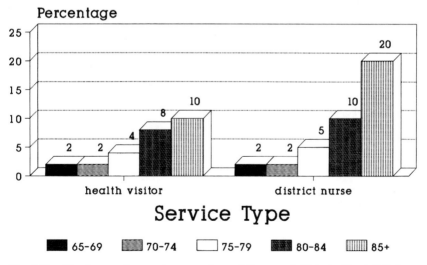

Fig. 7.12 Nursing service use by age of population aged 65 + in Great Britain, 1985.
Source: GHS (1985) – own analysis of unpublished data.

unresolved. Several studies have suggested that health visitors have a major role to play in screening and assessing the elderly (Luker 1988; Vetter *et al.* 1984). Health visitors are seen by their fellow health professionals as the group most suited to undertake this activity (Tremellen and Jones 1989). However, the same study revealed that at least half the health visitors surveyed saw the focus of their work being the 0–5 age group. This probably reflects the balance of their training where the emphasis is upon pre-school aged children. If a course includes an element concerned with older people it is usually from the perspective of geriatric medicine rather than gerontology, with its emphasis upon normal ageing.

Service utilization by 'vulnerable' groups

We have seen that all forms of medical care utilization increases with age. There are also gender differences in service use. How much are services used by two particularly 'vulnerable' groups, those living alone and those who are severely disabled as defined by a score of + on the Townsend index? With the exception of the GP, 1985 GHS data indicate that services reach only a minority of these two groups (Table 7.7). For example, GP home visits were reported by 78 per cent of the severely disabled and 35 per cent of those living alone. The coverage of the district nursing service was 31 per cent and 7 per cent respectively.

In the previous chapter we saw that there were social class differences in mortality and morbidity among the older age groups. Are these differences reflected in their patterns of service utilization? Crude medical service utilization rates are very similar for older people from across the spectrum of social classes (see Table 7.8). However, as illness is not equally distributed across the social classes it would appear that older people from manual occupations under-consult their GP. Using 1985 GHS data age, sex and disability, standardized consultation rates were calculated for the population aged 65 +. This exercise

Table 7.7 Utilization of health services by 'vulnerable' groups of population aged 65 + in Great Britain, 1985.

| | | % Using services | |
Service	Aged 85 +	Living alone	Severely disabled*
Hospital in-patient in last year	15	11	31
Hospital out-patient in last 3 months	15	17	28
GP consultation at home in last year	62	35	78
District nurse visit in last year	20	7	31
Health visitor visit in last year	10	6	17
N	265	1463	271

*Score of 7 + on Townsend index.
Source: GHS (1985) – own analysis of unpublished data.

Table 7.8 Utilization of health services by social class in population aged 65 + in Great Britain, 1985.

Service	%		Standardized service utilization rates*	
	Classes I & II	Classes IV & V	Classes I & II	Classes IV & V
Hospital in-patient in last year	13	12	101	99
Hospital out-patient in last 3 months	18	16	107	94
GP consultation at surgery in last 2 weeks	24	27	116	84
GP consultation at home in last 2 weeks	7	12	124	71
District nurse visit in last year	3	6	101	99
Health visitor visit in last year	5	5	99	101
N	824	985	—	—

*Standardized for age, sex and disability using indirect method.
Source: GHS (1985) – own analysis of unpublished data.

suggested that there were few class differences in community nurse use or acute hospital care. However, there does seem to be evidence that older people from professional and managerial backgrounds overconsume primary care services, especially home visits from GPs.

Conclusion and policy implications

Health services are used extensively by older people. Those aged 65 + account for approximately half of all expenditure on the NHS. They are the main consumer group for virtually every major medical specialism. Recently there has been a trend towards reducing length of stay for all patients, especially those in the older age groups. Financial constraints have forced hospitals to treat more patients more rapidly. These constraints are also forcing a reappraisal of the role of the hospital in the care of older people. Hospitals are, essentially, technologically sophisticated institutions geared towards crisis intervention. Is such a model of care appropriate to meet the needs of an increasingly old, and possibly frail, population? Clearly hospitals must respond to the changing patterns of disease with which they are going to be faced. The major medical specialisms must realize that the majority of their patients (consumers) are increasingly going to be elderly, with the resultant problems of frailty and multiple pathology. Consequently increased emphasis needs to be placed upon the role of assessment, rehabilitation and transfer rather than discharge back into the community. These changes would point to the need for more integrated care to meet the 'real' needs of older people. Will the changes in provision currently being put into place lead to greater integration or fragmentation?

8 PROVISION AND USE OF SOCIAL CARE

The 1989 Griffiths White Paper, *Caring for People*, made a key distinction between people with health care needs and those with social care needs. Although this distinction was not defined it is obvious that the Griffiths review was very much concerned with non-acute medical types of social care which would be provided in the community. In this chapter we briefly examine the development of community care policy; consider the Griffiths reforms and how they might affect the structure and organization of social service departments; and consider the role of formal and informal caring agencies.

Community care: the policy context

The post-war decades in Britain have seen a growing emphasis upon community as opposed to institutional provision for those groups in society requiring long-term care. Such groups include the elderly as well as those with mental illness or physical and/or mental handicaps. This trend is general to western Europe and North America. Across the range of western industrial societies there is a trend towards decreased institutional provision and a greater emphasis upon the care and maintenance of older people in their own homes for as long as possible. As the 1981 White Paper, *Growing Older*, commented 'care in the community must increasingly mean care by the community' (DHSS 1981, p. 3). In the field of care of the elderly it was stated that

> the primary objective of departmental policies . . . is to enable old people to maintain independent lives in the community for as long as possible. To achieve this high priority is being given to the development of domiciliary provision and the encouragement of measures designed to prevent or postpone the need for long term care in hospital or residential homes.
>
> DHSS 1978, p. 13

Thus, it is argued, care of the elderly is a responsibility which should be shared by all, and not one which solely involves statutory services. In this manifestation community care is seen as the responsibility of the family with state services only playing a rather residual role.

WHAT IS COMMUNITY CARE?

The origin of the term community care remains obscure. Bulmer (1987) observes that the first official use of the term was in 1957 and was related to the field of mental illness. In this context community care was taken to encompass both residential care and care which it was deemed appropriate for local health and social service authorities to provide in non-institutional settings. Walker (1982) comments that in this formulation community care implies support for the person by their friends, family and neighbours; an emphasis upon non-institutional forms of care, the provision of domiciliary statutory services and appropriate measures to prevent (re-) admission to institutional forms of care. However, over the decades, while the terminology has remained constant, the meaning of the term community care has undergone a subtle transformation.

It is possible to isolate several features of community care. In its original manifestation the term was used to mean care outside large institutions. In this sense the term may still be used in debates about the care of those who are mentally ill or handicapped. A second key element is the provision of services and care outside an institutional setting. Third is the idea of providing care in as normal i.e. non-institutional setting as is possible given the needs of clients. Fourth, there is a stress upon the involvement of members of the community in the care of those with long-term care needs. These multiple meanings given to the term community care result in a lack of precision and clarity. This makes it possible for governments of all political persuasions to argue in favour of this policy.

Bayley (1973) first suggested the useful distinction between care 'in the community' and care 'by the community'. Care in the community implies the use of statutory resources provided in clients' own homes; care by the community is associated with the mobilization of resources from within the community (voluntary organizations and informal carers such as friends, neighbours and kin). There are thus two main models of community care. First there is the notion of the community using its own resources to provide care via family and friends as well as voluntary and locally based formal services, and second there is the idea that the community's resources will be supplemented by those from external sources (e.g. national government). Increasingly in Britain statutory services are seen as being used as the last resort in the care of older people; the care of older people is being placed firmly within the domain of the family and the informal sector.

How are community care services currently organized?

As illustrated in the first chapter, formal community care services are provided by a variety of different agencies. The health sector provides community nursing, long-stay care and day hospital places as well as acute beds. Local authority social service departments are traditionally associated with the provision of domiciliary care services, typically home helps, as well as social work and residential care. The voluntary sector is also a provider of social care as are housing departments/associations and, increasingly, the private sector. It is obvious that the same types of care are being provided by a variety of different agencies. For any single client a variety of these actors are likely to be involved in their care and maintenance in the community; hence concerns among policy makers about coordination between agencies in the actual provision of care.

Community care: recent policy developments

There has been a broad consensus about the appropriateness of community care as a social objective. However, this has not been seen to be a very effective set of policies. So it has been subject to recent rigorous scrutiny by a series of government reports: the Audit Commission (1986), the House of Commons Social Services Committee Report (1985) and the Griffiths Report (1986) which resulted in the 1989 White Paper *Caring for People*.

THE AUDIT COMMISSION REVIEW

The Audit Commission review which was published in 1986 identified five main obstacles which they thought accounted for the slow and fragmented way that community care had developed in England and Wales. These were:

1 The different budgets maintained by health and local authorities which made the desired shift in resources from health to social services difficult to organize.
2 The lack of one-off finances to bridge the costs involved in moving from institutional to community care.
3 The use of social security benefits to fund private residential care which, it was suggested, offered an incentive towards institutional rather than community care. Following a small change in the rules for supplementary benefit provision elderly people claiming a supplementary pension were allowed to enter private residential care with the full cost being met by the state. This had resulted in a growth in the number of homes and a huge increase in the bill to the Exchequer. Subsequently the government 'capped' the amount of money it would pay in private care fees. This example

illustrates how one branch of government, through a minor change in welfare benefit regulations, has developed a policy in almost total opposition to the policy of community care being pursued by the health and social service agencies.

4 The problems resulting from bureaucratic difficulties due to differing geographical boundaries between health and social services, the non-compatibility of their organizational structures and divided and unclear responsibilities.

5 The inadequate training programmes which meant that there were inadequate staff to support the move from institutions to the community.

THE GRIFFITHS REVIEW

In December 1986 Mr Norman Fowler, the then Secretary of State for Health and Social Security, initiated a review of community care chaired by Roy Griffiths. The terms of reference for this enquiry were 'To review the way in which public funds are used to support community care policy and to advise on the options for action which would improve the use of these funds as a contribution to more effective community care'. This review may be seen as a follow up to the report by the Audit Commission (1986) and concern about the spiralling cost of social security payments to those in private residential/nursing home care noted above. The terms of reference for this review stated very clearly that the extent of resources being made available for community care was not being questioned. Rather the focus was again upon expending the money more judiciously.

The Griffiths Review concentrated upon adults who required care and support from others because they were elderly, mentally ill or handicapped or physically disabled (the so-called 'priority care groups'). The review was published in March 1988 as a Green Paper *Community Care: Agenda for Action* and resulted in the November 1989 White Paper *Caring for People*. The long gap between the publication of the Green Paper and the White Paper reflected the unpopularity among government circles of the main recommendations of the Green Paper.

THE COMMUNITY CARE WHITE PAPER: CARING FOR PEOPLE

This White Paper is based upon the assumption that for most people community care is the best form of care available. The ideology underpinning this report, therefore, promotes the ideals of the family as the main source of care and the home as the appropriate place to receive such care. There is a clear emphasis upon promoting the choice of individuals in influencing the type of care they receive, providing care outside institutions if at all possible and limiting the amount of care available so as not to foster dependence. This later point reflects the concern voiced by this administration to reduce the 'dependency culture' which they felt was promoted by universal and 'overgenerous' state welfare systems. With these objectives in mind the White Paper states that the proposed changes intended to:

1 Enable people to live as normal a life as possible in their own homes or in a homely environment in the community.
2 Provide the right amount of care and support to enable people to achieve maximum independence.
3 Provide people with greater say in how they live their lives and the services they need.

What is community care? As noted earlier, there has been a conspicuous failure upon the part of politicians in particular to say what they mean by the term. According to the White Paper community care may be defined as providing the right level of intervention and support to enable people to achieve maximum independence and control over their own lives. This requires the provision of a range of services.

What should community care consist of? The government identifies the key components of community as follows:

• Services which respond sensitively and flexibly to the needs of individuals and their carers.
• Services which allow a range of options for consumers.
• Services which do not intervene more than is necessary to promote independence.
• Services which concentrate upon those with greatest needs.

Six main objectives are indicated by the government for service delivery. These are stated as:

1 Promoting the development of domiciliary, day and respite services to enable people to live in their own homes.
2 Ensuring that services providers make support for informal carers a high priority.
3 Making proper assessment of need and good case management the key to the provision of good quality care.
4 Promoting the development of the independent sector.
5 Clarifying the responsibilities of agencies to increase accountability.
6 Securing 'better value for money'.

The White Paper goes into some detail as to how these objectives are to be achieved and it is beyond the scope of this volume to go over them in detail. It is, however, worth indicating that the paper does set specific priorities for 'elderly and disabled people'. This heading, which the report uses, is illuminating as it indicates that, for the government at least, old age and disability are synonymous. The priorities set are as follows:

- The promotion of positive lifestyles through health education, health surveillance, and screening to reduce the need for in-patient and residential care.
- The promotion of coherent networks of services which assist people to live dignified and independent lives in the community.
- The provision of a full range of services.
- The avoidance of unnecessary institutional care by assessment of need for care.
- Improved access to information about services at both local and national services.

The key recommendations of this White Paper were summarized briefly in the introduction. However, the main organizational and philosophical changes are briefly reiterated. First, there is the acceptance that elected local authorities, via their social services departments, should become the prime agency in developing community care with the responsibility for the publication of community care plans for their area, the assessment of individuals' needs for care, the purchasing of appropriate care and the inspection of all segments of the residential sector. Second, as with the health care sector, the government is attempting to develop a market for social care by separating the responsibility for those who purchase care and those who provide care. This will be achieved via the stimulation of the private and voluntary sector. In addition to their other responsibilities local authorities may still continue to be direct care providers if they so wish. Third, there will be a single unified social care budget which will cover all forms of care, either residential or domiciliary, purchased by local authorities. New entrants to private residential or nursing home care will not be funded via the social security system. There will be a single method of entry for those being supported by public funds irrespective of the type of institution (i.e. public, private, voluntary) which they wished to enter.

HOW WILL THESE AFFECT THE STRUCTURE OF SOCIAL SERVICE DEPARTMENTS?

There are significant variations in the way in which local authority social service departments are organized. However, we may identify, currently, two main styles of structure organized around either the functions provided by the department or the client groups served (see Figure 8.1). Many departments are also organized around the provision of services in a decentralized style within defined geographical locations, variously termed patches, localities, areas and sectors.

What will the post Griffiths review departments look like? While we cannot be certain about the precise structure it is clear that departments will have four main functions: assessment, purchasing of care, inspection of services and direct care provision (Figure 8.2). Furthermore, some of these parts of the organization

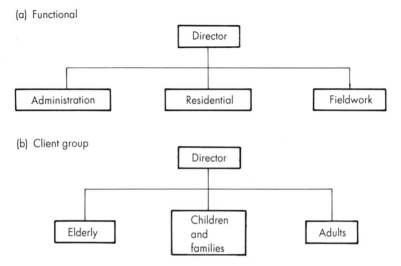

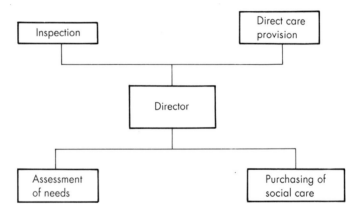

Fig. 8.1   Social services departments: pre-Griffiths structures.

Fig. 8.2   Social services departments: post-Griffiths functions.

will obviously no longer be working closely together. Cooperative relationships between sections will be, in theory at least, replaced by competitive ones. For example, those purchasing care cannot establish too close a relationship with the direct care providing groups. The inspection section must work at arm's length from the provider units, and so on. Implementation of this new social care providing system is, therefore, likely to radically affect the structure of social service departments and the relationship between its constituent elements.

Table 8.1   Expenditure on core community care services in Great Britain, 1987–88.

	£ (million)
Local authority domiciliary care:	
Home helps	535
Meals on wheels	59
Aids and adaptations	49
Day care (elderly)	77
Day care (other)	78
Adult training	167
Social work	202
Total	1167
Local authority residential care:	
Elderly	914
Others	269
Total	1183
Social security:	
Residential, nursing home residents income support	774

Source: Department of Health (1989b), Table 1.

How much do we spend on community care?

We expend a considerable amount of money upon the 'formal' community care services (Table 8.1). Of the £3124 million spent on community care a considerable amount is spent on older people; 63 per cent of all expenditure is spent on residential care.

Social care provision: the long-term care sector

Some older people, for a variety of reasons, require long-term care. In Britain long-term care is provided by three main sources:

1 Long-stay beds in the hospital sector.
2 Private/voluntary nursing and residential homes.
3 Residential accommodation provided by local authority social service departments.

Statutory responsibility for providing facilities for those elderly in need of care and attention is currently divided between the local authority (LA) and district health authority (DHA). Under Part 3 of the 1948 National Assistance Act LAs are required to provide residential accommodation for persons who, by reason of age, are in need of care and attention. The local authority can discharge this responsibility either by running or managing its own homes, known colloquially as 'Part 3 homes' or by sponsoring residents in homes provided by the private and voluntary sector. Long-stay care in hospitals is provided for the physically or mentally frail elderly. The provision of this form of care has its origins in the pre-war public hospitals, which had a large number of patients with chronic health care problems. Typically, long-stay hospital beds are located off the main DGH sites. This has tended to foster a very negative attitude towards this form of provision and the staff who work in such units. Typically such beds are located in pre-1914 hospitals, although the British Geriatric Society has consistently argued that they should be located in district general hospitals.

In the last decade the private sector has started to develop the amount of residential and nursing home care it provided. Some elderly people entering private care do so using there own financial resources. However, those in such care may, subject to their financial circumstances, claim public support from the social security systems to meet all or part of the charges. Up to 1980 the supplementary benefit regulations permitted claimants in residential homes who could not be catered for by the local authority an amount sufficient to meet reasonable board and lodging charges in the area. These were known as the local limit. Under the 1980 Social Security Act this system was maintained but local offices were given the discretion to pay in full the charges made by private and voluntary residential homes. In 1983 this was amended and a maximum payment ceiling established. This use of money from social security system to fund institutional care has created what has been termed 'a perverse incentive' to institutional rather than community care.

HOW MANY PLACES ARE AVAILABLE FOR LONG-TERM CARE?

As we saw in Chapter 2 approximately 5 per cent of those aged 65 + live in some form of institutional care. In 1985 there were approximately 272,817 people aged 65 + in long-term care (see Figure 8.3). This represents a 21.8 per cent increase in the numbers of elderly in residential care between 1980 and 1985 (see Figure 8.3). This increase was exclusively confined to the private sector which recorded a massive 115 per cent increase in the number accommodated. This increase in private care may reflect both the financial incentives to increase the number of places available and an increased demand for care brought about by an increasingly frail population and the decreased availability of domiciliary services. Why has the number of places offered by the public sector declined? This probably reflects a number of trends, including the switch to community provision, reduced numbers of places to provide residents with single rooms and limitations upon public sector expenditure.

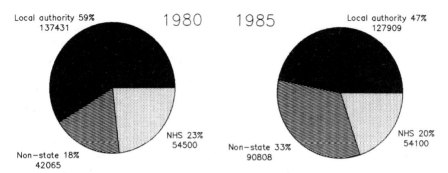

Fig. 8.3   Provision of long-stay care in England, 1980–85.
Source: Bosanquet and Gray (1989).

HOW MUCH IS SPENT ON PRIVATE LONG-STAY CARE?

The financial incentive created by the changed benefit regulations was obviously important in stimulating private enterprise because the number of elderly residents of private/voluntary homes receiving supplementary benefit increased by 104 per cent from 11,558 (1980) to 23,577 (1983). The amount of benefit paid increased from 18 million pounds in 1983 to about 1,000 million pounds in 1989.

ENTERING CARE

Attention has been given to predicting admission to long-term care because of concerns about the processes and mechanisms by which places are allocated. Policy makers are concerned to identify those 'at risk' of institutionalization so that appropriate community services can be developed to prevent/delay entry into an institution. Indeed, the whole Griffiths White Paper is centred upon reducing the amount of 'unnecessary' admission to institutional care. This, of course, raises the question of who defines an 'unnecessary' admission.

Several demographic variables are associated with admission to care. These are being very old, being female, living alone and being unmarried; this may reflect the lack of an informal care network for those in these demographic subgroups. These demographic variables are experienced in addition to high levels of physical dependence, frailty and mental health problems.

How is the decision to enter residential/nursing home care made? For entry into local authority residential care Sinclair (1988) observes that such decisions are made as a response to a crisis and that the idea of entering care rarely comes from the older person concerned. For the private sector Challis and Bartlett (1986) observed that about 60 per cent of admissions were the result of a crisis/emergency and again there appeared to be little choice of the actual home. Rather a home appeared to be selected upon the basis of availability rather than any other obvious criteria.

ENTERING CARE IN THE POST-GRIFFITHS ERA

The idea that people enter care 'wilfully' or 'inappropriately' enter institutional care does not seem to be borne out by the available data. It seems that most who enter care do so because there appears to be little alternative because they require high levels of care. Will the new community care scheme be able to provide such packages of care in the community? Once the community care reforms are implemented then entry into all forms of institutional care will be funded by the local authority only if an assessment indicates that it is the most 'appropriate' form of care for that individual. Of course those who can fund their own care will not have to be assessed before entry. When a case manager is assessing needs for care we might speculate whether, for those with intensive care needs, it might be 'cheaper' for care managers to opt for institutional rather than community provision.

When considering the notion of choice in relation to institutional care there are a number of different strands which require separate examination. First, there are ideas concerned with the choice of when an individual should enter care. Current evidence suggests that at the moment there is little 'choice' about when the time is 'right' to enter care. Will the Griffiths reforms change this? Second, there are issues about the choice of which home to enter, the locality of the home and how long to stay once care is entered. Again it is not clear, given the crisis-driven decisions about entering care, that any of these factors will come into play. It seems unlikely that the individual older person will have much greater say in the decision about entering care when the Griffiths reforms are implemented as the 'power' will be placed with the case manager not the older person.

THE CHARACTERISTICS OF THE INSTITUTIONAL POPULATION

As with other elements of gerontological research there has been a tendency to treat the institutional population as a homogeneous social group. The implicit but unstated assumption is that the various forms of provision, ranging from residential to long-stay geriatric care, are entirely substitutable. However, this is an untenable assumption and the institutional population illustrates a diverse population in terms of age, health status and needs, prognosis and expectation of life. Within any such population it is possible to identify four subgroups: long-stay residents; those who die shortly after admission, those who return home after a period of convalescence and those who move to another long-term care setting after a short stay. Any cross-sectional study of the nursing home/residential home population will over-represent to chronic long-term care population.

The institutional population, as Chapter 2 illustrated, is a very elderly population. Typically, residents of both public and private sector provision will contain a large number of people aged 80+. For example, studies in

Southampton (Lowrey and Briggs 1986) and Edinburgh (Capewell *et al.* 1986) have reported the average age of clients in care at about 83 years. The sex and civil status of residents varies within the different types of care. Nursing home residents are, in the survey from Edinburgh, predominantly female (90 per cent) and either single or widowed (98 per cent) (Capewell *et al.* 1986). Those in hospital long-stay provision include a larger percentage of men, about 32 per cent, and a higher number who are still married, about 16 per cent (Capewell *et al.* 1986). This suggests that those entering long-stay hospital care present different sorts of needs from those entering public/private nursing home or residential care.

A variety of different studies have illustrated that the distribution of dependency also varies within the long-term care sector (Bennet 1986; Harrison *et al.* 1990; Hodkinson *et al.* 1988). Direct comparisons between studies are problematic for the usual problems of varying methodologies. However, we can draw out some general conclusions. Physical frailty and disability varies across the different sectors, being least in public residential homes and highest in a hospital long-stay population. Private nursing homes have higher levels of frailty than residential homes but not usually as high as long-stay hospital care. For example, Bennet (1986) reports that the prevalence of urinary incontinence ranges from 73 per cent in a hospital long-stay population to 41 per cent in residential homes. However, although dependency and disability are high within the institutional population we must remember that a minority of the elderly have such problems. Even at the highest levels of disability the majority with these problems are resident in the community.

ATTITUDES TOWARDS INSTITUTIONAL CARE

Few researchers have, as yet, examined attitudes towards the institutional care sector. Salvage *et al.* (1989) examined attitudes towards residential care in a sample of those aged 75 + living in South Wales. Most respondents had heard of local authority homes (85 per cent) or geriatric hospitals (68 per cent). Knowledge levels about private sector homes were much lower. Approximately 20 per cent of subjects reported that they would be pleased to enter a private/public sector home, but only 10 per cent favoured the geriatric hospital. The perceived prime advantage of residential homes was being well cared for and companionship; the costs and loss of independence were perceived as the main disadvantages. For those who expressed interest in institutional care there was no clear statement in favour of either public or private care, although the geriatric hospital was unambiguously the least favoured option. However, overall institutional living was clearly not the favoured pattern of care for the majority of older people. These attitudes are probably not specific to the South Wales population studied as it seems among the population at large there is a general antipathy towards institutional care.

Care in the community: formal agencies

Different agencies offer domiciliary care in the community. The vast majority of day care is provided by the public sector, although the voluntary sector does make important contributions in some areas. Although there are many agencies operating in the domiciliary sector we have detailed utilization data for only a minority of these: home helps and the mobile meals services (meals on wheels). Typically the home help service has been characterized as being concerned only with home care rather than personal care. However, recent years have seen the development of the extended role of such services.

THE UTILIZATION OF FORMAL CARE SERVICES

In 1985 7 per cent of those aged 65 + were receiving home help services and 3 per cent home meals; this compares with 5 per cent and 1 per cent respectively in 1972. Clearly such services are being received by only a minority of elderly even in the very oldest age groups (see Figure 8.4). For example, 36 per cent of those aged 85 + receive home help services and 11 per cent receive meals on wheels. National data about the amount of care received are not available. However, levels of home care, in particular, are likely to be low. Even if we take two very vulnerable groups of elderly, those living alone and the severely disabled, then the coverage of these services remains far from universal (see Figure 8.5). There were no differences in the use of services by the social class of the older people. Both these services are well known amongst the older age groups and levels of satisfaction among users are high (Salvage *et al.* 1988). satisfaction among users are high (Salvage *et al.* 1988).

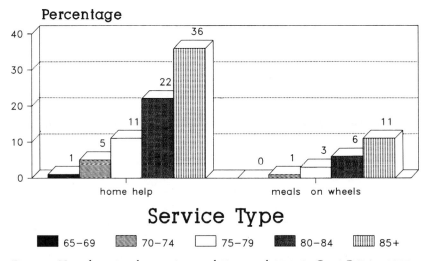

Fig. 8.4   Use of services by age in population aged 65 + in Great Britain, 1985.
Source: GHS (1985) – own analysis of unpublished data.

Percentage

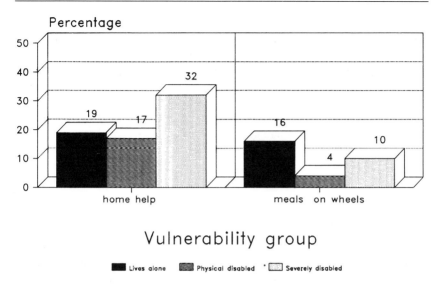

Vulnerability group

■ Lives alone   ▨ Physical disabled   *▨ Severely disabled

Fig. 8.5   Service use by 'at risk' groups of population aged 65 + in Great Britain, 1985.
*Score of 7 + on Townsend Index.
Source: GHS (1985) – own analysis of unpublished data.

DEVELOPING A MIXED ECONOMY OF DOMICILIARY CARE PROVISION

To date the private sector has been less important as a source of provision. However, it is an explicit aim of the White Paper to stimulate such care. How successful will this policy objective be? Clearly we cannot as yet give a definitive answer to this question. However, there are going to be difficulties in developing private care agencies. Will such businesses be sufficiently profitable to generate the interest of the private sector? There are obviously more overheads when the client group is geographically dispersed rather than grouped together in a home. How will private agencies oversee their staff? How will matters of training be addressed? How will older people receive the type, continuity and quality of care required? Many factors need to be addressed before the private sector will venture enthusiastically into this form of care provision.

Care in the community: the informal sector

First, we need to ask 'what is the informal sector?' This may be defined as care provided by family, friends and neighbours which is not organized via a statutory or voluntary agency and is not undertaken for financial reward.

Typically the term 'carer' is used to describe members of the informal sector who provide care for a dependent person in the community. The term 'carer' now has widespread currency in academic, policy making and lay circles. Yet this is a concept which was not in use a decade before (Arber and Ginn 1991). As these two authors indicate, 'carer' and 'caring' are emotive and value laden terms. The popular stereotype is that carers are perceived as a 'good thing', a group who are exploited by the state because their essentially unpaid labour forms the basis of current community care arrangements. A further image is that caring is a predominantly female experience; a typical caricature of a 'carer' would be that of a married middle-aged woman whose children had grown up and who was looking to re-enter the labour market.

THE RELATIONSHIP BETWEEN INFORMAL AND FORMAL CARE

Who is the main source of help for those older people who need help with the basic activities of daily living? Data from the 1985 GHS provides at least a partial answer to this question by providing information about who helped those older people who required assistance with a whole variety of adl tasks. Table 8.2 reproduces this information for a selected number of tasks concerned with mobility, personal care and housecare activities. With the exception of the cutting of toenails it is evident that the contribution of the informal sector far outweighs that of the formal sector. For example, of those who need help with shopping 85 per cent receive this from the informal sector.

Overall these data indicate that the informal sector is the main provider of help to older people, especially with the personal and household tasks which are required to maintain them in the community. This finding serves to refute the

Table 8.2   Provision of care to elderly people who need help with all activities in Great Britain, 1985.

Source of help	Steps and stairs	Personal care tasks	Cutting toenails	Shopping	Cleaning windows
Spouse	40	47	15	34	33
Other household member	24	39	5	16	15
Relative	21	8	6	18	11
Friend	3	1	—	8	2
Nurse/health visitor	2	4	2	—	—
Home help	—	1	—	7	19
Chiropodist	—	—	68	—	—
Paid help	—	—	—	1	12
Other	10	—	4	16	8
N	119	92	988	880	963

Source: GHS (1985) – own analysis of unpublished data.

powerful myth that older people are neglected by their family and that the main burden of caring for older people falls upon the state.

HOW ARE CARERS TO BE IDENTIFIED?

The first task in attempting to enumerate the extent and nature of informal care is to define what is meant by the term 'carer'. This task is by no means as simple as it sounds. We may take two approaches to the identification of this group. First, we can establish the prevalence of 'caring' by undertaking a survey of the general population. A second approach would be to identify a dependent population and then use this to identify their carers. The most extensive source of information about the nature and characteristics of informal carers is the OPCS survey (Green 1988). This was the first survey to attempt to study a nationally representative sample of those who were caring for the sick, elderly and handicapped, although there have been a variety of small local surveys and qualitative investigations of this topic. How did the OPCS survey identify carers? This study formed part of the 1985 GHS and informal carers were identified using two screening questions, which asked about extra family responsibilities resulting from looking after someone who was sick, elderly or handicapped in their own household (co-resident caring) or another household (non-resident caring) (see Table 8.3). The questions asked have a similar objective to many of those concerned with establishing the prevalence of a specific health problem; an attempt is being made to divide the population into two groups, those who are carers and those who are not. It remains unclear as to whether caring is so easily divided or whether, like morbidity, it is in fact a

Table 8.3 The prevalence of informal care in Great Britain, 1985.

	Male	% adults Female	All
1 Co-resident carers			
Some people have extra family responsibilities because they look after someone who is sick, handicapped or elderly. Is there anyone living with you who is sick, handicapped or elderly whom you look after or give special help to?	4	4	4
2 Extra-resident carers			
And how about people not living with you, do you provide some regular service or help for any sick, handicapped or elderly relative, friend or neighbour not living with you?	8	11	10
Percentage of adults who are carers	12	15	14
Estimated numbers of adults who are carers (millions)	2.5	3.5	6.0

Source: Green (1988).

continuum. Furthermore, the data derived from this study about caring is obviously dependent upon respondents' perception of their status as either carers or non-carers. The survey attempted to differentiate between caring and normal domestic labour by asking about 'extra' responsibilities. We can only speculate about how accurately respondents were (or were not) able to differentiate between these two categories and if they were differentially interpreted by men and women.

An example of the alternative approach is available from the work of Jones *et al.* (1983) and Qureshi and Walker (1989). Jones *et al.* used a sample of elderly resident in the community, identified those who required help with adl activities and then asked the older person to identify his or her 'main helper'. These carers were then followed up and details extracted about their caring responsibilities and the effects of caring. These various methodologies which have been used to study the issue of informal care are important for they help to reconcile some of the more important differences between surveys.

HOW MANY CARERS ARE THERE?

The only national data about the number of carers is available from the 1985 General Household Survey of this topic (Green 1988). This survey revealed that 4 per cent of adults reported that they looked after a dependant living in the same house (i.e. they were co-resident carer) with a further 10 per cent reporting that they looked after a dependant in another household (i.e. they were an extra-resident carer). Overall 15 per cent of adult females and 12 per cent of males defined themselves as carers. Grossing these responses up suggests that at least six million adults in Britain are carers and the majority, 75 per cent, are looking after a person aged 65 and over, 1.4 million adults provide care for more than 20 hours per week and 3.7 million have sole responsibility for the care of their dependant.

This key role of informal carers is recognised in the Griffiths White Paper which states 'the reality is that most care is provided by family, friends and neighbours'. However, the GHS estimate of six million carers is very much larger than 1.3 million suggested by Parker (1985). How is this large differential to be explained? Partly the differences reflect the varying methods. It is also due to the very wide way that the OPCS have defined caring. The definition does not, for very practical reasons, define caring in terms of time spent or the amount of time a dependant could be left for. Arber and Ginn (1991), when undertaking a secondary analysis of the OPCS data, drew a distinction between 'helping' and 'caring'. They argue that these are two distinct roles which are subsumed within the OPCS survey and that this accounts for the discrepancies identified. The main conclusion we may draw is that significant numbers of the adult population are actively involved in the care and assistance of older people. Further, the contribution of this sector is considerably in excess of the services provided by the state.

Table 8.4   Time spent providing informal care in Great Britian (%), 1985.

Hours per week	Co-resident carer	Non-resident carer
50 +	45	—
20–49	17	8
10–19	15	20
5–9	8	25
1–5	14	47

Source: Green (1988), Figure 4A.

HOW MUCH 'CARING' IS THERE?

Data from the GHS indicates that the time devoted by carers to their tasks is considerable (Table 8.4). Co-resident carers have a more extensive workload which reflects the more disabled nature of the dependent population and the definition of caring used in the study. Arber and Ginn (1991) estimate from these data that the average co-resident carer cares for 52 hours a week compared with 9 hours for an extra resident carer. Clearly those who live with their dependant are heavily committed to their task. The value of the work undertaken by informal carers is difficult to estimate with precision. However, if we ascribe a nominal value of £4 per hour to the work undertaken then informal carers as defined by the GHS undertake work to the value of £15,599–£24,041 billion per annum.

WHO IS A CARER?

How accurate is our stereotype of a carer as being a middle-aged woman? As with other social groups informal carers are not a homogeneous group. The GHS survey reported that two-thirds of carers were not living with their dependant. This contrasts with other surveys (Jones and Vetter 1984) which have indicated that at least two-thirds of carers were co-resident. This differential between studies again reflects the very generous definition of carers used by OPCS.

Another important subdivision of the informal caring population must be made concerning the relationship between carer and dependant. This largely distinguishes between spouses, who are likely to be men or women, and daughters (-in-law) (37 per cent). However, where the carer was non-resident cent of carers were spouses and 45 per cent were daughters (or daughters-in-law). Where the carer was co-resident they were either spouses (41 per cent) or daughters (-in-law) (37 per cent). However, where the carer was non-resident then it was usually the daughter or daughter-in-law (60 per cent). These findings appear to be representative of other studies concerned with carers of dependent elderly (Parker 1985; Qureshi and Walker 1989). These distinctions have implications for the type of care provided, the support services required and the stresses and problems associated with caring.

Several conclusions may be drawn from these data. First, the caring population is diverse but we may identify two main groups; spouse carers and children as carers. This distinction complicates debates about the gender-biased (or otherwise) characteristics of carers. Spouses as carers are equally likely to be male or female, whereas children as carers are almost exclusively female. Two points emerge from this. Caring is not an exclusive female preoccupation. As such a concentration upon 'women as carers' neglects the very important contribution of male carers (Arber and Gilbert 1989). Furthermore, many carers are themselves elderly. Consequently our obsession with the stereotypical middle-aged female carer is neglecting the important contribution of older people as contributors as well as recipients of care. We may develop this further. It is a feature of most surveys concerned with older people that they enumerate the care received by older people but rarely ask about the care that is provided by older people themselves.

WHAT ARE THE EFFECTS OF CARING?

Jones and Vetter (1984) investigated the effects of caring upon the 'quality of life' of the carer. This survey revealed that 11 per cent of carers had given up their job to care. Overall 16 per cent of carers felt that this reduced contact with their friends and 11 per cent reported reduced family contact. Such effects were reported more by co-resident as compared with extra-resident carers. More specifically, it was the daughters, as opposed to spouse carers, who were upset by the reduced social contact. Consequently they also illustrated higher rates of psychological anxiety and stress than spouse carers. Overall the effects of caring obviously vary considerably depending upon the relationship and residential relationship of carer and dependant.

BECOMING A CARER

The process whereby a family member takes on the role of informal carer is not fully understood. Indeed, it is very likely that the process varies with the relationship between the carer and dependant. For spouses it is probable that the entry into the carer-dependant relationship is influenced by the couple's previous marital history and relationship. For many couples 'caring' is seen as the culmination of the relationship and the natural conclusion of marriage ceremony vows. For daughters who take on the role the identification of the caring responsibility is probably much more complex and is related to a variety of factors including the services which are available, the needs of the older person, the type of relationship and feelings of filial responsibility.

Caring is usually depicted as a one-way relationship. Most surveys explore the type and amount of care provided to the older person. No account is usually taken of the care which the dependant may be giving or have given in the past to the carer. Thus such surveys ignore, for example, time spent in childminding of grandchildren and other such activities. The degree of reciprocity in the relationship is rarely thought an important issue to research. Yet it seems very likely that it is an important factor in explaining the caring relationship.

It is commonly asserted that older people prefer to receive care from family members rather than state agencies. This statement is difficult to refute or accept on the base of current research evidence. It is clear that older people value their independence and are reluctant to accept help. Available studies are divided about the attitudes of older people to accepting help from their children. A survey in South Wales indicated that two-thirds of older people supported the view that children should not be expected to look after their elderly parents. It seems unlikely, however, that older people are reluctant to accept care from their spouse.

Conclusions

The formal social care providing agencies are divided into various categories either by the type of agency involved, public or private or the location of care, institution or domiciliary. The services are used only by a minority of elderly. Further, few such services were ever designed to meet the needs of specifically elderly people. For example, the mobile meals services has its origin in the need to provide food to those whose homes had been destroyed by bombing during the war. Although there have been innovations in social care provision, which are outside the range of this book to review, there is still a tendency to fit people to services rather than vice versa.

Social care is being provided by a variety of different agencies. In terms of the size of the contribution, then, it is the informal sector which is the mainstay of community care. The situation is such that it is care *by* the community rather than care *in* the community. With or without the complicity of the government statutory services are performing a very limited role, However, we must not underestimate the potential role of services as it seems highly likely that propensity of the informal sector is enhanced rather than diminished by the support of statutory agencies.

There are debates about the future supply of informal care by families in future decades. It seems unlikely that there will be few changes in the supply of care between spouses. However, there are debates about the possible future role of children in providing care. Implicitly the notion of family care provided by daughters assumes a specific model of family life, most notably a stable nuclear family with a non-working female at home able to provide care. Divorce, decreases in family size and the increased labour market participation of women raise questions about future supplies of informal care. There is a further twist to the labour supply consideration. Many of those working in the formal care sector are women in low-paid jobs. Possible future labour shortages may also affect the formal care sector.

Although the White Paper states the importance of the informal sector there are few concrete proposals as to how this will develop. Carers generally operate alone rather than in a large network and, as noted earlier, they are not a single group. This has obvious policy implications. Carers must, like their dependants, be assessed as individuals and services developed which are appropriate to their needs.

Two further questions require consideration, if not resolution. Is community care cheaper than institutional provision and is community care a sexist policy? On the issue of cost the answer depends very much upon how the costs are calculated. If we exclude the contribution of the informal sector then community care may be 'a cheaper option'; if such costs are included or formal services are used extensively then community care is not a cheap option. This very important fact has not been accepted and community care is still seen as a way of getting 'care on the cheap'.

The issue about the sexist nature of community care is more complex. Certainly there are a large number of female carers and their availability to care is implicit within many policy documents. However, there are a significant minority of male carers who must not be excluded. It can be argued that community care still remains essentially sexist in that it assumes a large labour force of low-paid women to staff the formal sector. Whatever the gender of the person doing the caring it is clear that community care is a policy which is based upon the assumption that there is a pool of willing and able family members prepared to accept the role of 'informal carer'. Community care is being used as a euphemism for family care and it seems unlikely that recent policy developments will alter the basic pattern.

9 SOME ISSUES IN HEALTH AND SOCIAL CARE PROVISION

The passing of the NHS and Community Care Bill in June 1990 may result in the implementation of radical changes in the way in which health and social care is organized and delivered in future decades. In this section we consider the implications and possible effects upon older people of some of the major principles which underpin these changes. The new policies should be seen within such current areas of debate as the relationship between health and social care, the relative roles of central and local government, the relative roles of public and private care and the relationship between informal and formal care. Observation of the way health and social care is delivered in the coming decades will confirm the accuracy (or otherwise) of these speculative comments.

Health and social care: applying the philosophy of the market

As noted earlier, the NHS has, since its inception, been surrounded by almost continuous anxiety about rising expenditure levels. Hence in an attempt to 'improve efficiency' the service has been subject to periodic reviews involving managerial and organizational restructuring. The latest reforms are a continuation of this search to contain health (and, to a lesser extent, social care) expenditure. The creation of the NHS internal market and the mixed economy of social care represents the imposition of market principles to the two bastions of the British welfare state; this is, perhaps, the culmination of a decade of radical right-wing administration, which is committed to 'market philosophy'. The theory is that competition between those supplying care services will increase efficiency and thereby enable us to cope with the increased demand for such services.

An implicit but unstated background to this rising demand for care is the spectre of population ageing. Although the NHS White Paper refers coyly to rising demand the precise nature and origin of this demand is not specified. This fear is not unique to Britain, being widespread throughout the western industrialized world. How are state health systems to cope with the greying of the nation, which results in a seemingly insatiable demand for health and social care? The evidence presented earlier suggests that population ageing implies an increased demand for health and social care because of the greater morbidity of the older age groups. However, we must be cautious in drawing this inference because the vast majority of our information about morbidity in later life is derived from cross-sectional rather than longitudinal studies. Will future cohorts of elderly present with the same patterns of morbidity as today's generations? It could be argued that future cohorts will, because of greater affluence, better access to health care and an increased awareness of the importance of healthy lifestyles, present much lower levels of morbidity than those enumerated for the current population. Fries's optimistic thesis about the potential decreasing morbidity of future generations of elderly remains the subject of academic debate. Without the benefit of continuing longitudinal research it is impossible to answer these questions definitively.

The principle of the market draws a distinction between suppliers and consumers. However, for health and social care there is no such easy dichotomy. The 'demand' for health and social care is not generated solely by increasing numbers of consumers/patients but also derives from supply pressures generated by health care professionals and the pharmaceutical industry. Developments such as joint replacements or new drug therapies do not originate with patients but stem directly from the activities of the medical and pharmaceutical industries. It is unlikely that developments in either medical technology or the pharmaceutical industry will slow in the coming decades. How will these 'supply' and 'demand' factors be dampened by the introduction of a market-based system?

It was entirely in character for the administration which gave birth to these reforms to wish to apply the rationale of the market to the provision of health and social care. The decade from 1979 has seen the erosion of the post-war cross-party and national consensus on the provision of welfare services. Consistently the administration has sought to reduce the burden on the exchequer, to reduce the power of professionals and the state itself and encourage self-reliance. In a number of areas of welfare-related state activity such as housing, social services, social security, and now health and social care, these trends are clearly evident. The argument advanced is that state or local monopolies of care provision must be reduced if the autonomy and choice of the individual is to be maximized. There is a stress upon the values of individualism, freedom of choice and autonomy.

The NHS White Paper states two very explicit objectives which underpin the changes: (1) to provide patients with a better choice and (2) to give greater rewards to employees. Similar aims are stated for the community care reforms, which also stress the ubiquitous notion of 'value for money'. For both health and social care the assumption is that competition between providers will promote both better 'value for money' and services which are more responsive to the needs of consumers. Such statements are, however, simply assertions and we can only speculate as to what the effects of these changes will be. The development of the health and social care markets are intended to stimulate the involvement of private and voluntary care agencies and clearly reflect policy debates about the future role of state agencies. The role of state monopolies and the need to reduce their powers has been a clear policy theme of the current administration.

WHAT ARE THE IMPLICATIONS OF THE INTERNAL HEALTH CARE MARKET?

As the internal markets for health care are not fully implemented, we may only speculate about how these changes will affect older people (or indeed any other group within the population) as there are few countries which operate this type of system. In considering the changes we must distinguish between the primary and secondary health care aims of the health service. For GPs who opt to become budget holders then there are obvious incentives to remain within budget and avoid overspending. This is not surprising as such measures are an obvious attempt to impose 'cash limitations' upon the primary care service. As such this reflects the concern of the administration with reducing public expenditure and putting welfare services within specific budgetary frame-works. When considering health and social care changes it is important to place them within the ideological context of the administration which developed them.

What measures will GPs adopt to ensure that they remain within budget? We might speculate that primary care providers will become more selective in accepting patients or may, in extreme cases, attempt to remove certain 'expensive' patients from their lists. Which are the 'expensive' patient groups? Our analysis of primary care utilization illustrates that older people are high consumers and disproportionate users of services such as home visits. They are also significant users of prescribed medicines. One result of this may be that older people, especially those with multiple disabilities, may find it difficult to get access to primary care. The adoption of this policy within the family doctor service may well result in the further growth in the inverse care law: 'those who are in greatest need of care will be precisely the group which cannot get access to care'.

Further complications may arise from the desire of GPs to stay within budget. These could result in 'undertreating' patients because of a reluctance to refer patients to hospital, reduced consultation times or restricted prescribing. Although in numerical terms older people are important consumers of primary care services, there remain lingering suspicions that many of the diseases of later life are already undertreated, with the consequential abnormal pathology currently ascribed to 'ageing'. For example, signs of dementia or symptoms of incontinence may be attributed to old age when such conditions may result from, for example, an infection which could be easily treatable. Will such trends become more prevalent in a primary care system which is fundamentally concerned with remaining within budget?

Within the hospital sector the creation of the internal market is based upon an assumption that efficient hospitals will attract more patients and, as a consequence of this, additional resources. Much emphasis is placed upon this aspect of the internal market resulting in the expansion of 'successful provider units'. Little is made within the currently available documentation of the converse scenario: the demise of 'inefficient' hospitals. The logic of the proposals would be the bankruptcy of hospitals which were either unpopular, inefficient or both. Whether, given the significant capital investment which hospital development actually requires, rapid expansion (or contraction) of the hospital sector is possible remains a subject for debate. However, given the financial problems which beset the voluntary hospitals before the creation of the NHS hospital bankruptcy would seem a strong possibility.

How will older patients be affected by the internal market? Competition between providing units might result in a concentration upon services which are most 'efficient' and patient groups which are most 'profitable'. Indeed, the private hospital sector currently illustrates this approach with its concentration upon the niche market of elective surgery. Hospitals, especially the opted out NHS trusts, may no longer offer a full range of services as they seek to benefit from the economies of scale resultant from concentrating upon a few specialisms. This may lead to the demise of district general hospital services which are, in theory, offering a full range of services to the local resident population. The logic of the market may therefore result in reduced access to the full range of acute services for all age groups, not just those in the older age groups. Fragmentation of services and lack of continuity of care, which would adversely affect older people who often present a multiplicity of health problems, may be a further side effect of the emphasis upon competition. In a hospital service which is driven primarily by concerns with efficiency then the spectre of the bed blocking elderly patient is likely to loom even larger and there will be a continued stress upon reducing length of stay in hospital. Will such aggressive policies really result in improved care for older people?

SOCIAL PROVISION: DEVELOPING A MIXED ECONOMY OF CARE

Notions of the market are also an important part of the community care changes. A key element of the Griffiths community care reforms is the stimulation of non-state agencies in the provision of social care and the creation of a mixed economy of provision. The rationale for this stimulation of private and voluntary care provision agencies is the familiar maxim of increased choice, improved inefficiency as a result of competition between providers and services which are more responsive to the needs and wishes of consumers.

It is clear that there is some well justified dissatisfaction with the current way community care services are organized and delivered. In particular, concerns have been voiced about the fragmented way that care is provided and no clear and unambiguous set of objectives are stated for what we wish to achieve by community care. Current policies have also been deficient in addressing the needs and wishes of ethnic minority community members and informal carers. Will the development of a mixed economy of welfare in a market driven context address any of these questions?

As with the health care changes, the market philosophy assumes the expansion of 'popular' services and the contraction of unpopular providers. How will this be achieved without jeopardizing the care of some of the most vulnerable members of the community? Clearly, ensuring continuity of both social and health care is an element of the market-based system to which purchasers will have to give considerable thought. The current system does at least offer some certainty of service provision, if not the staff who actually provide the care.

The expansion of the private and voluntary care agencies raises issues as to how such agencies will be managed and staffed. Assuming that there is a growth in such services as a result of this policy development, where will such agencies find the appropriate staff? What types of vetting will they use to ensure that staff are appropriate for the tasks? Will such agencies spend time and effort developing and training care staff or will such 'optional extras' be dropped in order to reduce costs? Will this result in the public sector reducing training to remain competitive? Will the end result be that those working with older people will be the workforce with the lowest levels of training and skill?

It is an assumption of recent policy debates that state agencies cannot be responsive to clients' needs and wishes in the same way as services provided by the private sector. How legitimate is this assumption? Innovation in social care provision has, in the post-war period, been a feature of the public sector, as is evidenced by the Kent community care scheme. This debate about the future pattern of provision of community care services is, therefore, dominated by concerns with *who* should provide care; it pays much less attention to the equally crucial question of *what types* of care should be provided. Furthermore, consumers may not be interested in a sterile debate about who should organize care. What matters to older people is that they have greater accessibility to a high standard of care and that they do not wish to become involved in tangential debates on the merits (or otherwise) of the private or public sector.

Combating or continuing inequalities in care provision?

The creation of the National Health Service was intended to provide the country with a uniform level of access to both primary and secondary care services. A feature of the pre-NHS system had been very significant geographical inequalities in both the amount and quality of care available.

Despite all good intentions the current health and social care service is characterized by inequalities in levels and standards of care provided. However, reduction of these inequalities has, until recently, been stated as a majority policy objective. How will the trend to try to combat inequality be influenced by the creation of health and social care markets? We might speculate that the emphasis upon the market and local decision making would seem to suggest that inequalities will be increased by the demise of an at least token system of nation planning. Furthermore, if hospitals are allowed to go bankrupt in some districts or increase rapidly in others then clearly the principle of equality of geographical access will be breached. It would seem likely that those living in more remote rural areas might suffer under such a scenario; it seems unlikely that new services/hospitals would develop in rural locations with dispersed populations.

As well as geographical inequalities there are also socially based inequalities in access to care under the current system. Middle-class members of the population have benefited disproportionately from the services offered by the welfare state. Under the market-orientated system neither purchasers nor providers of care will be striving to reach those groups which fare badly under the current system. For example, who will be responsible for providing care to the homeless? Given the stress upon developing the independent sector and 'efficient' services it may well be that certain deprived social groups will find that their access to care is reduced. Will, for example, translated materials, translators, relevant diets be provided for the rapidly ageing British ethnic population?

Consumers, consumerism and choice

A key theme running through the reforms of the health and social service systems relates to the notion of consumerism and choice. Both the NHS and community care changes promote the ideology of increasing the choice of consumers over the type of care provided and increasing their influence over the services. Health and social care are being defined as goods or commodities which can be allocated via the mechanism of the market in much the same way as cars (goods) or insurance (services) are bought and sold. This approach assumes a dichotomy between producers and consumers of health and social care. But who are the producers of health and social care and who are the consumers?

When contemplating the purchase of an item the consumer surveys the market, compares prices and quality and, in theory at least, purchases the item which provides 'best value for money'. This model of the rational decision making consumer may be appropriate to the purchase of some goods or services but how well does it fit with the need to seek health of social care? Often the need for health care intervention is manifest in circumstances which threaten the life of an individual, who often has to rely on the skill and knowledge of the medical and nursing profession. Even if patients are not simply passive recipients of care, because of lack of knowledge it seems highly improbable that they will be able to adopt 'classic' consumer behaviour. How will the victim of a road traffic accident or a stroke be able to compare the price and quality of the medical and social interventions offered? If people require social care how will they be able to judge the merits of the potential sources available? Clearly in the new markets it will be the purchasing agents, not the patients, who are going to be those making the choices.

It is part of the consumerist philosophy that purchasers will not patronize those who provide poor quality services. How can patients or purchasing authorities enact this penalty upon the suppliers of 'faulty' or 'substandard' medical or social goods by failing to buy the services they provide? These comments would suggest that, despite the protestations of recent health and social care policy documents, clients (of whatever age) can be conceptualized as consumers in only the loosest and most non-rigorous of ways. The real consumers, who may have some impact upon the supply of care, are the purchasing agents (i.e. the health authorities or GPs), one step removed from the actual recipients of care.

Under the new system the power of the professions may well be reduced, to be substituted for by increased managerial strength; it is doubtful if older people will actually receive 'a greater individual say in how they live their lives and the services they need to do so'. None of the policy documents has any statement of the rights of older people (or indeed any other age group) with regard to access to the broad range of services and consultation in the types of care they receive. This is an important omission because many older people are often exposed to situations where other people take decisions, without consultation, on their behalf.

The Griffiths White Paper especially is very strong in emphasizing that the involvement of clients in the delivery of care is both straightforward, unproblematic and will be welcomed with open arms by statutory and non-statutory service providing agencies. However, it is a debating point as to whether such participation will be easy to achieve or welcomed by the agencies concerned. Advocacy and empowerment are obviously key themes underpinning especially the community care developments; but how willing will agencies be to give real power to older people (or other client groups)? What inducements will organizations have to include the views of clients? Do clients have the skills to participate and what incentives will there be for older people to participate? How will ideas about participation be expanded to include such groups as the elderly mentally ill? These questions are not intended to negate the ideas of advocacy and empowerment inherent in the community care document. Rather they serve to highlight the complexity of the issue and illustrate how easily the whole development could slip into political rhetoric, tokenism and sloganizing.

Community care versus institutional care

A central theme of British health and social policy in the post-war period has been the debate about the relative merits of community and institutional care. The Griffiths White Paper continues this debate and reiterates the now perceived wisdom that 'unnecessary' institutionalization should be avoided. Clearly the image conveyed is that care in the community is a 'good thing'. By contrast institutional care is perceived as therapeutically poor, highly inhumane and very costly. How accurate are these stereotypes? The assumed 'high quality' and humanity of care by the family, the actual reality of community care is contradicted by the evidence of so-called granny bashing. In contrast the Wagner Report (1988) indicated that great strides which have been made in improving the quality of residential care provided in the public sector. The stereotypes are, as ever, some way from the truth. Not all institutional care is bad and not all community care is wonderful. Our argument about the merits of various forms of provision would undoubtedly advance if we could shed our stereotypes.

It is assumed in the Griffiths changes that these two types of care are substitutable. Is this a valid assumption? Those currently entering care are highly dependent and typically lack an informal carer in whose absence community services cannot cope. Clearly such clients will require heavy input of care *if* they are to be maintained at home and this may prove more expensive than institutional care. How will the case manager reconcile the expenses of community care when dealing with a finite budget? How will the manager respond if the publicly funded older person wishes to enter care for 'social reasons'. Entry into care will, of course, not be vetted for those who are self-funded. A glib assumption that community and institutional care are easily substitutable for each other is clearly problematic.

It is unrealistic to expect that the requirement for institutional care can be completely eradicated. This means that there is a challenge to improve the type and quality of institutional provision, regardless of whether this is provided by the state, voluntary or private sector. Finch (1984) has challenged us to think positively about residential care and there are obviously many steps which could be taken by care providers to improve the quality of care. For example, relatives could make a positive contribution to care; the current system tends to exclude the family and does not permit them to contribute to the care of their relative in care. As well as improving the way older people in care are treated and the quality of their environment we could take steps to integrate residential care into the community and re-create 'normal' living in these communal settings.

Who should provide social care?

Clearly older people with an acute health problem require access to a skilled medical service. However, for the provision of social care there are important sets of issues which result from attitudes towards the giving and receiving of care. In the debate about the relationship between formal and informal care the community care documents are very clear in that they see the informal sector as the main and continuing frontline supporters of older people. Thus Griffiths (1988, p. 5) stated

> Publicly provided services constitute only a small part of the total care provided to people in need. Families, friends and neighbours and other local people provide the majority of care in response to needs which they are uniquely well placed to identify and respond to.

This sentiment reappeared in the White Paper as 'the great bulk of the care is provided by friends, family and neighbours' (DOH 1989b, p. 4). The state is being conceptualized as a residual provider of social care; community care is clearly being seen as care by the community.

Although the order of the players in the quotation is at variance with the research evidence, it is clear that the informal sector, and families specifically, are central to the care of older people. However, does the continued emphasis upon the key role of the informal sector actively reflect the needs and wishes of older people? There is now a growing body of research which suggests that older people state a preference for care by professionals rather than family members and that this preference is becoming more prevalent. In Norway Daatland (1990) has documented an increased preference amongst older people for state, as opposed to family, support. Similarly West et al. (1984) and Salvage et al. (1989) have both documented a clear preference for community-based professional care as opposed to either institutional or wholly informal care. Older people seem to be expressing a preference for care in the community rather than care by the community.

Little notice (despite their apparent claims) appears to be taken by current policy makers of these views of older people; indeed the recent policy developments ignore their attitudes totally. It is an implicit assumption of the Griffiths reviews that families will care for their older members because that is what families are for. However, Finch (1989) has indicated that care provision by the family is a complex entity built upon pre-existing relationships and biography. Support by family members to crisis and dependency is not automatic and is offered within a social context established over many years. To assume that future generations will offer (and wish to receive) the current types of care offered by families is a huge assumption which fails to recognize the changing nature of family structures.

The past decade has been characterized by a plethora of research and debate, much of it stemming from the activities of feminists, illustrating the nature of informal care. There is a consensus among academics and, to some extent, policy makers that community care imposes a 'burden' upon women. Foster (1990) poses the intriguing question as to why this piece of feminist-inspired research has been ignored and suggests that this is because the research described a situation that policy makers felt was perfectly appropriate. Indeed, despite all the rhetoric the Griffiths White Paper does not in any way specifically address the issue of gender inequalities in informal care; these are implicitly accepted as 'natural'! Indeed, despite its protestations the report is not at all specific as to how informal carers are to be sustained and nurtured.

The situation is further complicated by changing demography as well as structural factors. Reductions in family size will reduce the pool of daughters who are one of the main providers of informal care. Changing views about the role of women in society have resulted in 'informal care' being seen as less of an 'obligation' for this group. As Rossiter and Wicks (1982) observes, the notion of family care implies a particular model of family life (an elderly person living with or near to his or her family; a stable nuclear group and a middle-aged woman at home financially supported by a spouse) which is becoming almost extinct. Given these trends is it legitimate to build a whole set of policies around the continued emphasis upon the role of the informal sector?

Assessing the need for care: case management

Another central theme of both community care and NHS White Papers is the emphasis upon the assessment of need and the targeting of resources to those most 'in need'. The community care White Paper sets out the idea that case management is the legitimate method of fulfilling this policy objective. However, the White Paper offers few guides as to how case management will work in practice and there are aspects of this notion and that of 'needs assessment' and the 'targeting of resources' which merit further debate.

What is meant by the term need? Very briefly, need may be defined as the ability to benefit from a health or social care service. We may further subdivide need into three main categories: met need, unmet need (i.e. an insufficiency of services provided) and overmet need (i.e. the overprovision of care). Further, we may distinguish between population and individual measurement of need. The Griffiths reforms envisage a system of need assessment; but how this will be achieved is unclear, especially as the proposed care system distinguishes between those with complex needs and those with simple needs. Considerable thought will have to be given to how the system for the assessment of need will be devised. Implicit in the reforms is a 'filtering mechanism' so that only those most 'in need' will be allocated a case manager. Who will undertake this filtering? What criteria will be used? Will these, and the main needs assessment protocol, be standardized across the country?

Who should undertake the function of case management? The White Paper is not prescriptive on this but rather suggests a whole range of different professional groups who might take on this role. Phillipson (1990) observes that much of the debate has focused upon who should be the case manager. He interprets this as a reflection of the trend for professional groups to be concerned with who should control resources rather than engaging in more fundamental scrutiny of policy development.

What is case management? The concept is not defined in the White Paper. However, we may distinguish two main types of case management; the advocacy and gate keeping approaches. Case management as advocacy focuses upon clients and centres upon brokerage activities by concentration upon the design and implementation of care plans by coordinating existing services. The gate keeping manifestation of case management is where case managers have access to cash-limited budgets within which they must remain. The White Paper conceptualization of case management is clearly within the cost containing, cash-limited, gate keeping manifestation.

There are a number of important practical issues which require attention if case management, in whatever guise, is to become a central feature of the British social care system. Clearly there is a significant training aspect to the development of a large number of case managers. How will these new workers be given the advocacy and financial skills which they will undoubtedly require? What tools will be used to assess the case needs of individuals? In the case of conflict whose needs will count most? Those of the dependent elderly person or their informal carers? Case managers are obviously going to be key players in the new scheme. Will older people be able to challenge the resultant assessment? Clearly there are both philosophical and practical issues which require confrontation if an effective system of case management is to be developed.

There is also potentially an important conflict between the assessment, advocacy and financial activities of the case manager. If the case manager is a budget holder then there is a tension between his or her role in assessing needs for care and responsibility as holders of a finite and cash-limited budget. How will case managers reconcile their conflicting tension? What mechanisms will be established to ensure that assessments are based upon client needs and not the state of the case manager's budget? Will the client assessed at the end of the financial year get the same treatment as one seen at the start of the year? Clearly such issues must be addressed if older people, and other client groups, are to be able to look forward to an equitable and effective system of social care.

Paying for care

An explicit feature of the NHS White Paper was the exemption from income tax for private health insurance premiums for retired people. This is very clearly an attempt to drive older people from the public sector. This is complemented in the Griffiths reforms by a directive that the full ability of those receiving social care to pay for this should be assessed. There is a clear policy switch towards promoting the ability of older people to pay for the care received. This policy assumes, of course, that older people have sufficient disposable income to purchase private health insurance or other forms of social care. Much has recently been made of the increasingly affluent character of the older age groups. However, the available data illustrates that older people are by no means affluent and are concentrated in the bottom 20 per cent of the income distribution. In comparison with the rest of society few elderly people have sufficient financial resources to pay for health care, even assuming that health insurance companies would offer cover to this age group. Premiums for private health insurance for older people are high. This reflects the increased probability that such groups will need care. In 1990 premiums per month for private health insurance for those aged 65–74 range from £15.30 to £39.58, for those aged 75 the range is £23.60 to £52.46. Premiums are adjusted twice yearly and rarely cover the home nursing or long-term care that older people often require. Few elderly people have sufficient income to pay such high premiums. Despite the growth of home ownership, there will be a significant minority, 40 per cent, who do not have the ability to realize such an asset to pay for their care. Developing policies which are based upon the ability of older people to pay are, therefore, fatally flawed unless pensions are to be radically increased in value.

Purchasing care: costs and quality

Central to the proposed changes is the notion that competition between providers of health and social care services will drive down 'prices' and so produce better value for money. For those purchasing care upon what basis will 'value for money' be measured? Implicit in this term is the concept of purchasing the most effective service (i.e. most therapeutically beneficial and highest quality) at the lowest price. How will such variables be measured? Currently it is difficult to establish the true 'cost' of many health and social care services and almost impossible to identify their effectiveness or quality. Unless there is a radical change in information systems then it looks suspiciously as if services will be purchased on the basis of price alone. Cheapest is not always best and efficient services do not necessarily offer high quality.

The measurement of the quality of care being offered is problematic as this is a multi-faceted concept which may be considered at a variety of levels of analysis: the purchaser, the care recipient and the provider. For care purchasers quality may be considered in rather global terms such as, for example, infection rates after elective surgery. For consumers measures of quality may be related to the way they experience the care received, such as the quality of the food, the cleanliness of the ward or the punctuality of the staff, while for providers professional standards will be clearly important.

Measuring the quality of care is obviously far from simple. However, one way in a system of care which is driven by the market are the measures that purchasers may introduce into their contract. For example, acute hospitals units may be required to produce discharge plans for all older people or may be penalized if they discharge a person aged 75 + on a Friday night who lives alone. Clearly contracts do have some potential for raising quality; but it will require a complex monitoring procedure to see that these results arise.

Funding health and social care

The NHS is currently funded from three main sources; taxation (86 per cent), national insurance contributions (11 per cent) and charges (3 per cent) (Ham 1985). The White Paper does not envisage any change to the basic funding structure; it envisages that the majority of funding will continue to come from taxation. However, there is a stress upon hospitals improving patient facilities, especially in hotel aspects such as single rooms, and charging 'extra' for this. Does this mean a two-tier service might be created, with those who can pay enjoying luxurious facilities and those who cannot be consigned to low standard, poorly provided for, public wards. If such a scenario were to materialize then it is likely that older people, who are least able to pay, will 'enjoy' the worse accommodation during their hospital stay.

There has been a lively debate about whether the money allocated by central to local government via the standards spending assessment for community care should be 'ring fenced'. Indeed the House of Lords forced an amendment to this effect. This would mean that local authorities could not use the money for other purposes. This strategy and the House of Lords amendment was rejected by the government. Furthermore, it is not possible to consider how effective this new system of social care provision will be without any hint as to the size of the budget. The whole issue of funding community care is interrelated with the introduction of the poll tax. Most predictions indicate that the cost of implementing these reforms will be high. This raises problems for the government's desire to reduce the level of poll tax bills in the country in the run up to a general election, and illustrates how the issue of community care has formed part of the debate about the relationship between central and local government. The financial aspect of the community care reforms will obviously be crucial to their successful implementation. The most likely scenario at the moment is that the amount of money provided will not be sufficient to meet all the 'needs' generated and it may well turn out that public funds will be expended on only a small number of very dependent people, with other clients being left to their own resources.

Conclusion

The use of blanket terms such as 'the elderly', 'the retired' and 'old people' conveys an image of a homogeneous social group devoid of internal social divisions and differences. This is, perhaps, one of the most enduring of all stereotypes of old age. From a policy perspective the persistence of this stereotype promotes and maintains the view that a monolithic policy response is appropriate to respond to the need of older people; one policy will fulfil everyone's needs and expectations.

Two different concepts are contained within this stereotype. The first suggests that all older people are the same. This is difficult to support intuitively as 'the elderly' may include an age range 65–105. We could not lump together all people aged 20–64 and try to argue that they are a single social group. Why do we do this for the older age groups? A second image is that dimensions of stratification such as class and gender, which are so important in differentiating the non-elderly, are of no importance to the older age groups. Upon entry to old age factors such as ethnicity and class are no longer important in differentiating the population.

This image is not an accurate representation of older age groups and later life. As has been shown elsewhere older age groups are very diverse. Dimensions of social stratification such as class (Victor 1989), gender and ethnicity exert a profound influence on the experience of ageing. In examining health in later life, and in the provision of health and social care, careful attention should be given to these dimensions. Old age is not a homogeneous experience.

The demographic data illustrate that there will be an increasing number, although not necessarily percentage, of older people in the British population. Population ageing is not, however, confined to Britain but is a feature of most western industrial countries. One reason why population ageing is viewed so negatively is that an old population is seen as an unhealthy population. As we have seen the prevalence of chronic health problems increase with age. However, predicting the health status of future generations of older people is speculative as future cohorts may not illustrate the same patterns of mortality and morbidity as today's.

The passing of the NHS and Community Care Bill suggests that the pattern of health and social care provision will be radically altered in the coming years. Working from an assumption that the main problems with the pattern of care provision are organizational, the changes envisaged are essentially managerial. Central to the reforms is the separation of the funders and providers of care and the creation of health and social care and 'a mixed economy' of care provision operating along market principles. The current systems of care provision are by no means perfect and require considerable changes. However, they do attempt, especially for health care, to provide a universal system which is accessible, equitable and acceptable to all members of the population. It is not obvious that the changes will uphold these principles; consequently future generations of older people may be confronted with worse health and social care services.

REFERENCES

Acheson, D. (1988). *Public Health in England: The Report of the Committee of Inquiry into the Future Development of the Public Health Function*. HMSO: London.

Adelstein, A. M., Downham, D. Y., Stein, Z. and Susser, M. (1968). 'The epidemiology of mental illness in an English city', *Social Psychiatry*, **3**, 47–59.

Alderson, M. R. (1988). 'Demographic and health trends in the elderly', in Wells, N. E. J., and Frear, C. (eds). *The Ageing Population: Burden or Challenge*, Macmillan: London.

Alderson, M. R. and Ashwood, F. (1985). 'Projection of mortality rates for the elderly', *Population Trends*, **42**, 22–36.

Almind, G., Frear, C., Gray, J. A. M. and Warshaw, G. (1983). *The contribution of the primary care doctor to the medical care of the elderly in the community*, Institute of Gerontology: Ann Arbor, MI.

Ames, D., Ashby, D., Mann, A. M. and Graham, N. (1988). 'Psychiatric illness in elderly residents of Part III homes in one London borough: prognosis and review'. *Age and Ageing*, **17**, 249–56.

Andrews, I. R. (1986). 'Relevance of readmission of elderly patients discharged from geriatric unit.' *Journal of American Geriatric Society*, **34**, 5–11.

Arber, S. and Gilbert, G. N. (1989). 'Men: the forgotten carers', *Sociology*, **23**, 1:111–18.

Arber, S. and Ginn, J. (1991). 'The meaning of informal care: gender and the contribution of elderly people'. *Ageing and Society*, forthcoming.

Atchley, R. C. (1977). *The Social Forces in Later Life: An Introduction to Social Gerontology* Wadsworth Belmont: CA.

Audit Commission (1986). *Making a Reality of Community Care*. HMSO: London.

Barber, J. M. and Wallis, J. B. (1976). 'Assessment of the elderly in general practice', *Journal of the Royal College of General Practitioners*, **26**, 106–14.

Barnard, M. (1988). 'Taking charge – strategies for self-empowered health behaviour among older people', *Health Education Journal*, **47**, 2/3:87–8.

Bayley, M. J. (1973). *Mental Handicap and Community Care*. Routledge & Kegan Paul: London.

Bedford, A., Foulds, G. A. and Sheffield, B. F. (1976). 'A new personal disturbance scale DSSI/SAD'. *British Journal of Social and Clinical Psychology*, **15**, 387–91.

Bennet, J. (1986). 'Private nursing homes: contribution to long-stay care of the elderly in Brighton Health District', *British Medical Journal*, **293**, 867–9.

Binney, E. A. and Estes, C. L. (1988). 'The retreat of the state of its transfer of responsibility: the intergenerational war', *International Journal of Health Services*, **18**, 1:83–90.

Black, S. E., Blessed, G., Edwardson, J. A. and Kay, D. W. K. (1990). 'Prevalence rates of dementia in an ageing population: are low rates due to the use of insensitive instruments?' *Age and Ageing*, **19**, 84–90.

Blaxter, M. (1983). 'The causes of disease: women talking', *Social Science and Medicine*, **17**, 56–69.

Blaxter, M. (1990), *Health and Lifestyles*. Tavistock Routledge: London.

Blessed, G., Tomlinson, B. E. and Roth, M. (1968). 'The association between quantitative measures of dementia and of senile changes in the cerebral grey matter of elderly subjects', *British Journal of Psychiatry*, **114**, 797–811.

Blessed, G. and Wilson, I. D. (1982). 'The contemporary natural history of mental disorder in old age', *British Journal of Psychiatry*, **141**, 59–71.

Bond, J. and Carstairs, V. (1982). *The Elderly in Clackmannan*, Scottish Health Service Studies, no. 42, Scottish Home and Health Department: Edinburgh.

Bond, J., Gregson, B. A., Atkinson, A. and Newell, D. J. (1989). 'The implementation of a multi-centred randomized controlled trial in the evaluation of the National Health Service Nursing Homes', *Age and Ageing*, **18**, 96–102.

Bosanquet, N. and Gray, A. (1989). 'Will you still love me? New opportunities for health services for elderly people in the 1990s and beyond', *National Association of Health Authorities (NAHA) Research Paper* No. 2, NAHA: Birmingham.

Brayne, C. and Ames, J. (1988). 'The epidemiology of mental disorders in old age', in Gearing, B., Johnson, M. and Heller, T. (eds), *Mental Health Problems in Old Age*. Open University Press: Milton Keynes.

Broe, G. A. Atchtar, A. J., Andrews, G. R., Caird, F. I., Gilmore, A. J. and McLennan, W. S. (1976). 'Neurological disorders in the elderly at home', *Journal of Neurology*, **39**, 4:361–6.

Bulmer, M. (1987). *The Social Basis of Community Care*. Unwin Hyman: London.

Bury, M. (1988). 'Arguments about ageing, long life and its consequences'. in Wells, N. and Freer, C. (eds), *The Ageing Population: Burden or Challenge?* Macmillan: Basingstoke.

Calasanti, T. and Bonanno, A. (1986). 'The social creation of dependency, dependency ratios, and the elderly in the United States: a clinical analysis', *Social Science and Medicine*, **23**, 12:129–36.

Capewell, A. E., Primrose, W. and MacIntyre, C. (1986). 'Nursing dependency in registered nursing homes and long-term care geriatric wards in Edinburgh', *British Medical Journal*, **292**, 1719–21.

Central Statistical Office (CSO) (1989). *Social Trends*, 19. HMSO: London.

Central Statistical Office (CSO) (1990). *Social Trends*, 20. HMSO: London.

Central Statistical Office (CSO) (1991). *Social Trends*, 21. HMSO: London.

Challis, L. and Bartlett, H. (1986). *Old and Ill: Private Nursing Homes for Elderly People*. Age Concern/Institute of Gerontology Research Paper, no 1. Age Concern: London.

Christie, A. B. (1985). 'Survival in dementia: a review', in Arie, T. (ed.), *Advances in Psychogeriatrics*. Churchill Livingstone: Edinburgh.

Clarke, M., Clarke, S., Odell, A. and Jagger, C. (1984). 'The elderly at home: health and social status', *Health Trends*, **16**, 3–7.

Clarke, M., Lowry, R. and Clarke, S. (1986). 'Cognitive impairment in the elderly: a community survey', *Age and Ageing*, **15**, 278–84.

Coid, J. and Crome, P. (1986). Bed Blocking in Bromley. *British Medical Journal*, **292**, 1253–6.

Coleman, P. (1988). 'Mental health in old age', in Gearing, B., Johnson, M. and Heller, T., *Mental Health Problems in Old Age*. Open University Press: Milton Keynes.

Copeland, J. R. M., Dewey, M. E., Wood, N., Searle, R., Davidson, I. A. and McWilliam, C. (1987). 'Range of mental illness among the elderly in the community', *British Journal of Psychiatry*, **150**, 815–23.

Copeland, J. R. M., Kelleher, M. J., Kellett, J. M., Gourlay, A. J., Gurland, B. J., Fleiss, J. L. and Sharpe, L. (1976). 'A semi-structured clinical interview for the assessment of diagnosis and mental state in the elderly. The geriatric mental state schedule – development and reliability', *Psychological Medicine*, **6**, 439–49.

Cox, B. D., Blaxter, M., Buckle, A. L. J. and Fenner, N. P. *et al.* (1987). *The Health and Lifestyle Survey*, The Health Promotion Research Trust: London.

Cumberlege Report (1986). *Neighbourhood Nursing: A Focus of Care; Report of the Community Nursing Review*. HMSO: London.

Daatland, S. O. (1990). 'What are families for?' *Ageing and Society*, **10**, 1–15.

Dale, A., Evandrou, M. and Arber, S. (1987). 'The household structure of the elderly population in Britain', *Ageing and Society*, **7**, 37–56.

Davidson I., Dewey M. E. and Copeland, J. R. M. (1988). 'The relationship between mortality and mental disorder: evidence from the Liverpool longitudinal study', *International Journal of Geriatric Psychiatry*, **3**, 95–8.

De Beauvoir, S. (1985). *Old Age*. Penguin: Harmondsworth.

Department of Health and Social Security (DHSS) (1978). *A Happier Old Age*. HMSO: London.

Department of Health and Social Security (DHSS) (1980). *Inequality in Health* (the Black Report). HMSO: London.

Department of Health and Social Security (DHSS) (1981). *Growing Older*. HMSO: London.

Department of Health and Social Security (DHSS) (1984). *Population, Pension Costs and Pensioners' Income*. HMSO: London.

Department of Health and Social Security (DHSS) (1986). *Community Care: Agenda for Action*. HMSO: London

Department of Health and Social Security (DHSS) (1987). *Promoting Better Health*. HMSO: London.

Department of Health (DOH) (1989a). *Working for Patients*. HMSO: London.

Department of Health (DOH) (1989b). *Caring for People*. HMSO: London.

Department of Health (DOH) (1989c). *Health and Personal Social Service Statistics 1989*. HMSO: London.

Doyal, L. (1979). *The Political Economy of Health Care*. Pluto Press: London.

Eisdorfer, C., Mullner, R. and Cohen, D. (1989). 'The role of the hospital in the care of older people'. in Ory, M. G. and Bond, R. I. (eds), *Ageing and Health Care*. Routledge: London.

Estes, C. L., Gerard, L. E., Zones J. S. and Swan, J. H., (1984). *Political Economy, Health and Ageing*. Little Brown: Boston.

Estes, C. and Binney, E. A. (1988). 'Toward a transformation of health and ageing policy', *International Journal of Health Services*, **18**, 1:69–82.

Evans, J. G. (1983). 'Integration of geriatric with general medicine services in Newcastle', *Lancet*, **1**, 1430.

Falkingham, J. (1987). 'The demographic characteristics of Britain's aged population'. *Research Note No. 7*. Welfare State Programme STICERD: LSE.

Falkingham, J. (1989). 'Dependency and ageing in Britain: a re-examination of the evidence'. *Journal of Social Policy*, **10**, 2:211–33.

Fentimen, I. S., Tirelli, U., Monfardi, S., Schneider, M., Festen, J., Coynetti, F. and Aapro, M. S. (1990). 'Cancer in the elderly: why so badly treated?', *Lancet*, **335**, 1020–22.

Fiegehen, G. (1986). 'Income after retirement', *Social Trends*, **16**, 13–18, CSO, HMSO: London.

Finch, J. (1984). 'Community care: developing non-sexist alternatives', *Critical Social Policy*, **9**, 6–18.

Finch, J. (1989). *Family Obligations and Social Change*. Policy Press: Cambridge.

Finch, J. and Groves, D. (1983). *A Labour of Love*. Routledge & Kegan Paul: London.

Fletcher, A. (1990). 'Screening for cancer of the cervix in elderly women'. *Lancet*, **335**, 97–9.

Foster, P. (1990). 'Community care and the frail elderly: a feminist rethink', Paper presented at Social Policy Association Annual Conference, Bath, July.

Foulds, G. and Bedford, A. (1979). *Manual of the Delusions – Symptoms – States Inventory*. NFER Nelson: Windsor.

Fox J., Jones, D., Moser, I. R. and Goldblatt, P. (1985). 'Socio-economic differences in mortality', *Population Trends*, **40**, 10–16.

Fries, J. E. (1980). 'Ageing, natural death and the compression of morbidity'. *New England Journal of Medicine*, **303**, 3:130–35.

Fries, J. E. and Crapo, L. M. (1981). *Vitality and Ageing*. Freeman: SF.

Gaspar, D. (1980). 'Hollymoor hospital dementia service: Analysis of outcome of 230 consecutive referrals to a psychiatric hospital dementia service', *Lancet*, **1**, 1401–5.

Gee, E. M. and Kimball, M. M. (1987). *Women and Ageing*. Butterworths: Toronto and Vancouver.

Gee, E. M. and Veevers, J. E. (1983). 'Accelerating sex differentials in mortality: an analysis of contributing factors', *Social Biology*, **30**, 75–85.

Gilmore, A. (1977). 'Brain failure at home', *Age and Ageing*, **6**, 56–60.

Grahan, M. and Livesley, B. (1988). 'Can readmissions to a geriatric unit be prevented?', *Lancet*, **1**, 404–6.

Green, H. (1988). *Informal Carers*. OPCS series GHS No. 16. OPCS, HMSO: London.

Griffiths, R. (1988). *Care in the Community: Agenda for Action*. HMSO: London.

Griffiths, R. A., Good, W. R., Watson, N. P., O'Donnell, H. F., Fell, P. J. and Shell, J. M. (1987). 'Depression, dementia and disability in the elderly', *British Journal of Psychiatry*, **150**, 482–93.

Gruenberg, E. M. (1977). 'The failures of success', *Millbank Men Fund Quarterly*, **55**, 1:3–24.

Gruer, R. (1975). *Needs of the Elderly in the Scottish Borders*, Scottish Health Service Studies No. 33, Scottish Home and Health Dept: Edinburgh.

Guillermard, A. M. (1982). *Old Age, Retirement, a Social Class Structure in Ageing a Life Course*, Translated and edited by T. K. Marevena and K. J. Adams, Guildford: NY.

Gurland, B., Copeland, J., Kuriansky, J., Kelleher, M., Sharpe, L. and Dean, L. L. (1983). *The Mind and Mood of Ageing: The Mental Health Problems of the Community Elderly in New York and London*. Croom Helm: Beckenham.

Ham, C. (1985). *Health Policy in Britain* Macmillan: London.

Harrison, R., Savla, N. and Kafety, K. (1990). 'Dementia, depression and physical disability in a London borough: a survey of elderly people in and out of residential care and implications for future developments', *Age and Ageing*, **19**, 97–103.

Hedstrom, P. and Ringen, S. (1987). 'Age and income in contemporary society: a research note', *Journal of Social Policy*, **16**, 2:227–39.

Henderson, A. S. (1990). 'The social psychiatry of later life', *British Journal of Psychiatry*, **156**, 645–53.

Henderson, A. S. and Kay, D. W. K. (1984). 'The epidemiology of mental disorders in the aged', in Kay, D. W. K. and Burrows, G. D. (eds), *Handbook of Studies on Psychiatry and Old Age*. Elsevier: Amsterdam.

Hepple, J., Bowler, I. and Bowman, C. (1989). 'A survey of private nursing home residents in Weston-Super-Mare', *Age and Ageing*, **18**, 61–3.

Herzlich, C. (1973). *Health and Illness*. Academic Press: London.

Hodkinson, E., McCafferty, F. G., Scott, J. M. and Stout, R. W. (1988). 'Disability and dependency in elderly people in residential and hospital care', *Age and Ageing*, **17**, 147–54.

Hoover, S. L. and Siegel, J. S. (1986). 'International demographic trends and perspectives on ageing', *Journal of Cross Cultural Gerontology*, **1**, 5–30.

Horrocks, P. (1982). 'The case for geriatric medicine as an age-related specialty', in Isaacs, B. (ed.), *Recent Advances in Geriatric Medicine*, Vol. 2. Churchill Livingstone: Edinburgh.

House of Commons Social Services Committee (1985). *Community Care*, Vol. 1, report HC13-1, session 84/85. HMSO: London.

Hunter, D. J. and Judge, K. (1988). *Griffiths and Community Care: Meeting the Challenge*. King's Fund Institute, briefing paper No. 5. King Edward's Hospital Fund for London: London.

Ineichen, B. (1987). 'Measuring the rising tide: how many dementia cases will there be by 2012?', *British Journal of Psychiatry*, **150**, 193–200.

International Labour Office (1989). *From Pyramid to Pillar*. ILO: Geneva.

Jagger, C., Clarke, M. and Cook, A. J. (1989). 'Mental and physical health of elderly people: five-year follow-up of a total population', *Age and Ageing*, **18**, 77–82.

Johnson, P. (1988). *The labour Force Participation of Older Men in Britain 1951–81*. Centre for Economic Policy Research, Discussion paper No. 284. CEPR: London.

Johnson, P., Conrad, C. and Thomson, D., (eds) (1989). *Workers Versus Pensioners: Intergenerational Justice in an Ageing World*. Manchester University Press, Manchester.

Jones, D. and Vetter, N. J. (1984). 'A survey of those who care for the elderly at home: their problems and needs', *Social Science and Medicine*, **19**, 5:511–14.

Jones, D. A., Victor, C. R. and Vetter, N. J. (1983). 'Carers of the elderly in the community', *Journal of the Royal College of General Practitioners*, **33**, 707–10.

Jones, D., Victor, C. R. and Vetter, N. J. (1984). 'Hearing difficulty and its psychological implications for the elderly', *Journal of Epidemiology and Community Health*, **38**, 75–8.

Jones, D., Victor, C. R., and Vetter, N. J. (1987). 'Visual disability and associated factors in the elderly', *Health Visitor*, **60**, 256–7.

Jorm, A. F., Korten, A. and Henderson, A. S., (1987). 'The prevalence of dementia: a quantitative integration of the literature', *Acta Psychiatrica Scandinavia*, **76**, 465–79.

Kalache, A., Warnes, A. M. and Hunter, D. J. (1988). *Promoting Health among Elderly People*, King Edward's Hospital Fund for London: London.

Kaplan, G. A. (1987). 'Mortality among the elderly in the Alameda County study: behavioural and demographic risk factors', *American Journal of Public Health*, **77**, 307–12.

Kaplan, G. A. and Haan, M. M. (1989). 'Is there a role for prevention among the elderly? Epidemiological evidence from the Alameda County study', in Ory, M. G. and Bond, K. (eds), *Ageing and Health Care*. Routledge: London.

Kay, D. W. K., Beamish, P. and Roth, M. (1964). 'Old age mental disorders in Newcastle upon Tyne part I: a study of prevalence', *British Journal of Psychiatry*, **110**, 146–58.

Kay, D. W. K., Berymann, K., Foster, E. M., McKechni, A. S. and Roth, M. (1970). 'Mental illness and hospital usage in the elderly: a random sample followed up', *Comprehensive Psychiatry*, **11**, 26–35.

Kover, M. G. (1986). 'Expenditures for the medical care of elderly people living in the community', *Milbank Memorial Fund, Quarterly*, **64**, 100–32.

Kramer, M. (1980). 'The rising pandemic of mental disorders and associated chronic diseases advisabilities', *Acta Psychiatrica Scandinavica*, **285**, 62 (supplement), 382–97.

Laing, W. and Propper, C. (1990). 'Prospects for the elderly consumer in the 1990s', STICERD Welfare State Series Seminar, LSE, May.

Laslett, P. (1989). The demographic scene in Eetcelaar, J. and Pearl, D. (eds). *An Ageing World: Dilemmas and Challenges for Law and Social Policy*. Clarendon Press, Oxford, 3–24.

Leathard, A. (1990). *Health Care Provision: Past, Present and Future*. Chapman and Hall: London.

Lewis, J. and Meredith, B. (1988). *Daughters Who Care*. Routledge: London.

Lowrey, S. and Briggs, R. (1986). 'Boom in private rest homes in Southampton: impact on the elderly in residential care', *British Medical Journal*, **296**, 541–3.

Luck, M., Lawrence, B., Pocock, B. and Reilly, K., (1988). *Consumer and Market Research in Health Care*. Chapman and Hill: London.

Luker, K. A. (1988). 'The nurse's role in health promotion', in Wells, N. and Frear, C. (eds), *The Ageing Population*. Macmillan: London.

McAuley, W. J. (1987). *Applied Research in Gerontology*. Van Nostrand Reinhold: New York.

McNab, A. and Phillip, A. (1980). 'Screening an elderly population for psychological well-being', *Health Bulletin*, **38**, 160–5.

Mann, A. M., Graham, N. and Ashby, D. (1984). 'Psychiatric illness in residential homes for the elderly: a survey in one London borough', *Age and Ageing*, **13**, 257–65.

Manton, K. G. (1982). 'Changing concepts of mortality and morbidity in the elderly population', *Millbank Memorial Fund Quarterly*, **60**, 183–244.

Martin, J., Meltzer, H. and Elliot, D. (1988). *The Prevalence of Disability Amongst Adults*: OPCS, HMSO: London.

Martyn, C. N. and Pippard, E. C. (1988). 'Usefulness of mortality data in determining the geography and time trends in dementia', *Journal of Epidemiology and Community Health*, **42**, 134–7.

Maule, M., Milne, J. S. and Williamson, J. (1984). 'Mental health and physical health in older people', *Age and Ageing*, **13**, 349–56.

Millard, P. (1988). 'New horizons in hospital based care', in N. Wells and C. Frear (eds), *The Ageing Population, Burden or Challenge*. Macmillan: London.

Milne, J. S. (1985). *Clinical Effects of Ageing*. Croom Helm: London.

Morgan, K., Dallosso, M., Arie, T., Byrne, D. J., Jones, R. and White, J. (1987). 'Mental health and psychological well-being among the old and very old living at home', *British Journal of Psychiatry*, **150**, 801–7.

Mossey, J. M., Havers, B. and Wolinstay, F. D. (1989). 'The consistency of formal health care utilization', in Ory, M. G. and Bond, I. R. (eds), *Ageing and Health Care*, Routledge: London and New York.

Muir Gray, J. A., (1985). 'Education for health in old age' in Muir Gray, J. A., (ed.), *Prevention of Disease in the Elderly*. Churchill Livingstone: Edinburgh.

Mullner, R., Read, W. and Kralovec, P. (1987). 'Trends in hospital services for the aged', Paper presented at the 1987 Public Health Conference on Records and Stats, Washington DC.

Murphy, E. (1982). 'Social origins of depression in old age', *British Journal of Psychiatry*, **141**, 135–42.

National Audit Office (NAO) (1987). *Community Care Development*. HMSO: London.

Office of Population, Census and Surveys (OPCS) (1987). *Hospital Inpatient Enquiry: 1986*, OPCS: London.

OPCS (1988a). *General Household Survey 1985*, OPCS: London.

OPCS (1988b). *General Household Survey 1987*, preliminary results, GHS Monitor SS/88/2, OPCS: London.

OPCS (1989a). *Mortality Statistics: Serial Tables 1841–1985*. DMI No. 19, OPCS: London.

OPCS (1989b). *Mortality Statistics: England and Wales: Cause 1987*, OPCS: London.

Organisation for Economic Cooperation and Development (OECD) (1988). *Ageing Populations: The Social Policy Implications*. OECD: Paris.

Ouslander, J. G. and Beck, J. C., (1982). 'Defining the health problems of the elderly'. *Annual review of Public Health* **3**, 55–83.

Parker, G. (1985). *With Due Care and Attention*. Family Policy Studies Centre: London.

Parker, R. A. (1987). *The Elderly and Residential Care: Australian Lessons for Britain*. Gower, Aldershot.

Parker, S. (1980). *Older Workers and Retirement*. HMSO: London.

Pattie, A. M. and Gilleard, C. J. (1975). 'A brief psychological assessment schedule – validation against psychiatric diagnosis and discharge from hospital', *British Journal of Psychiatry*, **12**, 489–93.

Pattie, A. M. and Gilleard, C. J. (1976). 'The Clifton Assessment Schedule – Further validation of a psychogeriatric assessment schedule', *British Journal of Psychiatry*, **129**, 68–72.

Pattie, A. M. and Gilleard, C. J. (1979). *Manual of the Clifton Assessment Procedures for the Elderly (CAPE)*, Hodder and Stoughton: Sevenoaks, Kent.

Phillipson, C. (1982). *Capitalism and the Construction of Old Age*, Methuen: London.

Phillipson, C. (1990). *Delivering Community Care Services for Older People: Problems and Prospects for the 1990s*. University of Keele, Centre for Social Gerontology, Working Paper No. 3.

Pill, R. and Stott, N. (1982). 'Concepts of illness causation and responsibility', *Social Science and Medicine*, **16**, 42–52.

Pill, R. and Stott, N. (1985). 'Choice or chance: further evidence on ideas of illness and responsibility for health', *Social Science and Medicine*, **20**, 981.

Primrose, W. R. and Capewell, A. D. (1986). 'A survey of registered nursing homes in Edinburgh', *Journal of the Royal College of General Practitioners*, **36**, 125–8.

Qureshi, H. and Walker, A. (1989). *The Caring Relationship*. Macmillan: London.

Rorsman, B., Hagnell, O. and Lantie, J. (1986), 'Prevalence and incidence of senile and multi-infarct dementia in the Lundby study: a comparison between the time period 1947–1957 and 1957–1972', *Neuropsychobiology*, **15**, 122–9.

Rossiter, C. and Wicks, M. (1982). *Crisis or Challenge. Family Care, Elderly People and Social Policy*, Study Commission on the Family: London.

Royal Commission on the National Health Service (Merisson Report) (1979). HMSO: London.

Salvage, A. V., Vetter, N. J. and Jones, D. A. (1988). 'Attitudes to hospital care among a community sample of people aged 75 and older', *Age and Ageing*, **17**, 270–4.

Salvage, A. V., Vetter, N. J. and Jones, D. A. (1989). 'Opinions concerning residential care', *Age and Ageing*, **18**, 380–6.

Schneider, E. L. and Brody, J. A. (1983). 'Ageing, national death and the compression of morbidity: another view', *New England Journal of Medicine*, **309**, 854.

Scott, P. and Johnson, P. (1988). *The Economic Consequences of Population Ageing in Advanced Societies*. Centre for Economic Policy and Research, Discussion Paper No. 286.

Sinclair, I. (1988). 'The elderly', in Sinclair, I. (ed.), *Residential Care: The Research Reviewed*. HMSO: London.

Slater, R. and Gearing, B. (1988). 'Attitudes, stereotypes and prejudice about ageing', in Gearing, B., Johnson, M., and Heller, T. (eds), *Mental Health Problems in Old Age*. Open University: Milton Keynes.

Smith, A. and Jacobson, B. (eds) (1988). *The Nation's Health*. King Edward's Hospital Fund for London: London.

Taylor, R., Ford, G. and Barber, J. M. (1983). *The Elderly at Risk: A Critical Review of Problems in Screening and Case Finding*, Age Concern England: Mitcham.

Thompson, E. G. and Eastwood, M. (1981). 'Survivorship and senile dementia', *Age and Ageing*, **10**, 29–32.

Tinker, A. (1984). *The Elderly in Modern Society*. Longman: London.

Townsend, P., Phillimore, P. and Beattie, A. (1988). *Health and Deprivation: Inequality and the North*, Croom Helm: Kent.

Tremellen, J. and Jones, D. A. (1989). 'Attitudes and practices of the primary health care team towards assessing the very elderly', *Journal of the Royal College of General Practitioners*, **39**, 142–4.

Tudor-Hart, J. (1971). 'The Inverse Care Law', *Lancet.*

Tulloch, A. J. and Moore, V. (1979). 'A randomised controlled trial of geriatric screening and surveillance in general practice', *Journal of Royal College of General Practitioners,* **29**, 733–42.

van der Heuvel, Wim J. A. (1988). 'Balanced health and health care for the elderly', in Schroots, J. J. F., Birren, J. E. and Svanborg, A. (eds), *Health and Ageing: Perspective and Prospects.* Springer: N.Y.

Verbrugge, L. M. (1989). 'Gender, ageing and health', in Markides, K. S. (ed.). *Ageing and Health.* Sage: Newbury Park, CA.

Vetter, N. J., Charny, M., Farrow, S. and Lewis, P. (1988). 'The Cardiff health survey: the relationship between smoking habits and beliefs in the elderly', *Public Health,* **102**, 359–64.

Vetter, N. J. and Ford, D. (1989). 'Anxiety and depression scores in elderly fallers', *International Journal of Geriatric Psychiatry,* **4**, 159–63.

Vetter, N. J., Jones, D. A. and Victor, C. R. (1984). 'Effect of health visitors working with elderly people in general practice: a randomised control trial', *British Medical Journal,* **288**, 369–72.

Vetter, N. J., Jones, D. A., Victor, C. R., and Philip, A. E., (1986). 'The measurement of psychological problems in the elderly in general practice', *International Journal of Geriatric Psychiatry,* **1**, 127–34.

Victor, C. R. (1983). *A Survey of the Elderly After Discharge from Hospital,* PhD thesis, Welsh National School of Medicine.

Victor, C. R. (1987). *Old Age in Modern Society* Croom Helm: Beckenham.

Victor, C. R. (1989a). 'Income inequality in old age', in Jeffrys, M. (ed.), In *Growing Old in the Twentieth Century.* Routledge: London.

Victor, C. R. (1989b). 'Health inequality in later life', in McQueen, D. V. and Hunt, S. (eds), *Readings for a New Public Health,* EUP: Edinburgh.

Victor, C. R. (1990a). 'What is health? A study of the health beliefs of older people', *Journal of the Institute of Health Education,* **28**, 1:10–15.

Victor, C. R. (1990b). 'A survey of the delayed discharge of elderly people from hospital in an inner-city health district', *Archives of Gerontology and Genetics,* **10**, 199–205.

Victor, C. R. and Vetter, N. J. (1985a). 'The early readmission of the elderly to hospital', *Age and Ageing,* **14**, 37–42.

Victor, C. R. and Vetter, N. J. (1985b). 'A one year follow-up of patients discharged from geriatrics and general medical units in Wales', *Archives of Gerontology and Geriatrics,* **4**, 117–24.

Victor, C. R. and Jefferies, S. (1990). 'The readmission of elderly people to hospital in an inner-city health district', *Archives of Gerontology and Geriatrics,* **10**, 89–95.

Wagner, G. (1988), *Residential Care: A positive choice.* HMSO: London.

Waldron, I. (1976). 'Why do women live longer than men?', *Social Science and Medicine,* **10**, 349–62.

Walker, A. (ed.) (1982). *Community Care: The Family, State and Social Policy.* Basil Blackwell & Martin Robertson: Oxford.

Walker, A. (1985). 'Early retirement: release or refuge from the labour market?', *Quarterly Journal of Social Affairs,* **1**, 211–29.

Wall, R. (1988). *Leaving Home and Living Alone: Historical Perspective.* CEPR discussion paper No. 211. CEPR: London.

Wenger, G. C. (1984). *The Supportive Network.* Allen & Unwin: London.

West, P., Illsley, R. and Kelman, H. (1984). 'Public preferences for the care of dependency groups', *Social Science and Medicine,* **18**, 4:417–46.

Whitehead, M. (1987). *The Health Divide: Inequalities in Health in the 1980s.* Health Education Authority: London.

Williams, R. (1983). 'Concepts of Health: an analysis of lay logic', *Sociology*, **17**, 185–205.

Williams, R. (1990). *A Protestant Legacy*, Clarendon Press: Oxford.

Williamson, J., Stokoe, I. H., Gray, S. and Fisher, M. *et al.* (1964). 'Old people at home: their unreported needs', *Lancet*, **i**, 1117–20.

World Health Organisation (WHO) (1989) *Health of the Elderly*, WHO: Geneva, (Technical Series Report 779).

INDEX

243038